PROPERTY OF LYNN APPLETON

ONE STOP Property

The One Stop Series

Series editor: David Martin, FCIS, FIPD, FCB
Buddenbrook Consultancy

A series of practical, user-friendly yet authoritative titles designed to provide a one stop guide to key topics in business administration.

Other books in the series to date include:

David Martin	*One Stop Company Secretary*
David Martin	*One Stop Personnel*
Jeremy Stranks	*One Stop Health and Safety*
John Wyborn	*One Stop Contracts*

1997 titles:

David Martin	*One Stop Property*
Robert Leach	*One Stop Payroll*
Harris Rosenberg	*One Stop Finance*
Karen Huntingford	*One Stop Insurance*
David Martin/ John Wyborn	*One Stop Negotiation*
Robin Ellison	*One Stop Pensions*

ONE STOP
Property

DAVID MARTIN

ICSA Publishing
*The Official Publishing Company of
The Institute of Chartered Secretaries and Administrators*

First published 1997 by
ICSA Publishing Limited
Campus 400, Maylands Avenue
Hemel Hempstead
Hertfordshire, HP2 7EZ

© David Martin, 1997

All rights reserved. No part of this publication may be reproduced, stored in a retrieval system, or transmitted, in any form, or by any means, electronic, mechanical, photocopying, recording or otherwise, without prior permission, in writing, from the publisher.

Typeset in 10/12.5 pt Meridien with Frutiger Light
by Hart McLeod, Cambridge

Printed and bound in Great Britain
by Hartnolls Ltd, Bodmin, Cornwall

British Library Cataloguing in Publication Data

A catalogue record for this book is available from the British Library

ISBN: 1-86072030-7

1 2 3 4 5 01 00 99 98 97

Contents

Preface	vii
Access	1
Acquisition – financial	9
Acquisition – general	15
Advertising hoardings	21
Archiving (plans, permissions, consents, etc.)	23
Assignment	27
Building regulations	31
Building works	33
Condition, Schedule of	39
Contaminated land	43
Contingency planning	45
Covenants	51
Dilapidations, Schedule of	59
Disposal	63
Duties of property administrator	67
Environment protection	69
Fire procedure	73
Fire certificate	75
First Aid	77
Fitting out	81
Freehold	87
Guarantees	91
Health and Safety	93
Insurance	103
Internal rent	111
Landlord and Tenant Act	113
Leasehold	117
Lessee's works	121
Licence	123
Long-term planning	125

Maintenance planning	129
Marriages of interests	135
Neighbour relationships	137
Notices	141
Obtaining value	145
Occupier's Liability	149
Options to break	153
Payments	157
Planning applications	161
Précis	165
Privity of contract	169
Property Register	171
Rating	177
Reinstatement	181
Relocation – general	183
Relocation – personnel implications	189
Rent confidentiality agreements	193
Rent – paying and collecting	195
Rent free periods	199
Rent review	201
Rent review memorandum	213
Rent review submissions	215
Rental evidence	223
Repairs and redecorations	225
Risk assessment and prevention	227
Service charges	233
Surveys	235
Tenancy agreement	237
Termination	243
Terrorist Action	247
Toilet facilities	251
Trespassers	253
Underletting	255
Use and user clause	257
Valuations	261
Case references	263

Preface

During a recent survey of the UK's top 1000 companies, a leading firm of surveyors found that only 20% of those questioned had a comprehensive data base covering the properties they occupied, whilst the records of 10% were so incomplete that not even addresses were recorded centrally. Experience indicates that in only very few companies is control of what may be a business's most valuable assets represented at board level.

The reality is that in most organisations property matters and obligations are overlooked and the responsibility for the enormous range of complex requirements is allocated to a manager, a supervisor or a secretary who already have full-time responsibilities in other areas. This book – the distillation of 30 years of property administration and 10 years presenting seminars to those responsible for property – should answer some of the questions they may have on the topic.

Inevitably in a book of this size, one cannot give chapter and verse on the subject (the attention of those readers who require greater detail is drawn to the ICSA loose-leaf manual The Administration of Property) but my purpose here is to provide a practical, user-friendly guide which may well answer 90% of the questions of those with responsibility for, but without formal training in, property administration.

The book uses the expanded index format in presenting content on a subject-by-subject basis with limited cross-referencing. This leads to some duplication of content which is deliberate in order that each item can be treated comprehensively under its own title.

Finally, although guidance and advice are provided here, the point is made repeatedly in the text that very often, an initial assessment of a problem or opportunity has been made. The way forward may be to take specialist advice. In commissioning such advice, this book should allow the reader to pose the correct questions and show some comprehension of the scope of the problems!

David M Martin
Buddenbrook
June 1997

Note
The description 'Lessee' (rather than 'tenant') has been used in this book to emphasise the responsibilities of this party under the lease which conveys rights but entails such responsibilities.

Access

Introduction

Whilst every occupier of property wishes to allow access to their property (and may be required by law to grant access to certain regulatory bodies), control needs to be exercised over such access in the interests of security, safety and confidentiality.

Those gaining access can be divided into five categories.

1. Those who are employed at and/or are required to visit the premises in the ordinary course of business.

2. Those who own the business (for example, shareholders) who have a number of statutory rights of access – mainly to inspect certain records.

3. Members of the public and creditors of limited companies who have statutory rights of inspection of certain records.

4. Representatives of official bodies who are entitled to gain access under authority vested by statute, contract, etc.

5. Those who have no right to be there but who may trespass for their own purposes. (Occupiers and owners may still have obligations to TRESPASSERS despite, presumably, being totally opposed to their presence.)

1. Employees and visitors

The most numerous of those requiring access to an organisation's property are employees and visitors who have some relationship with the organisation and/or with the goods or services being produced. Whilst few organisations would wish to place any restrictions on such access, there may be occasions when restrictions on access to the premises and/or to 'sensitive' areas of the premises may be essential. It may be preferable to set this out in a procedure such as the following so that employees are aware of such requirements. This is particularly relevant to computer departments and to those organisations vulnerable and attractive to TERRORIST ACTION, or to industrial espionage, which tends to be more widespread than is often realised. Installing electronic access equipment may not only solve some of the security problems referred to here but may also provide an attendance record and input to payroll which may be particularly valuable where wages are calculated on an 'hours worked' basis.

Access procedure

(a) Employees can only gain access to the premises of the organisation using the electronic card keys in the externally sited mechanisms adjacent to the entrances. A card (with a personal access number) will be issued on commencement of employment. The use of an individual's card is restricted to the particular employee to whom it was issued. The card must also be inserted in the control mechanism on every occasion on which an employee leaves the premises.

(b) If an employee loses his or her card, the fact must be reported to the personnel administrator (or equivalent) immediately and a new card obtained. In the event of second or subsequent replacement cards being required, the company reserves the right to charge for these.

(c) All non-employees will be stopped at the Gatehouse and directed to Reception. All visitors will be requested to complete the visitors' book in Reception, following which each will be given a visitor's badge to be worn at all times in the building and surrendered on leaving.

(d) Managers, etc., receiving a visitor(s) are responsible for escorting them throughout their visit and ultimately back to Reception, for recovery of the visitor's badge, and for signing the visitor(s) out.

(e) Near the end of the normal working day, Reception will check the status of current visitors and make arrangements concerning their exit after Reception is locked. The employee responsible will escort such visitors to the night exit, collect the visitor's badge, return it to Reception and book the visitor out.

(f) Reception staff are responsible for keeping the visitors' book up to date, replacing full pages when necessary, ensuring badges are returned, checking discrepancies, and reporting them to the property or personnel administrator (PA).

(g) Employees who wish to arrange a site visit for members of their family, or for members of a school or other organisation, should apply to the PA giving full details of the organisation, numbers involved, etc. Visits are restricted to one each month, so it may be necessary to book such a visit well in advance. All members of such a party visiting the premises are subject to the rules that apply to employees, must keep to the

ACCESS

designated routes, wear appropriate clothing and observe all necessary safety and other rules.

(h) Children under the age of 12 are not normally allowed in the plant. Employees who require children to attend the plant (e.g. to await the end of a shift being worked by a parent/guardian/relative) should make arrangements with the PA for the child(ren) to wait in the [specify] department. Employees are fully responsible for the actions of their child(ren) whilst on the premises, and the organisation will accept no liability arising as a result of this concession.

Internal theft

Should there be evidence or strong suspicions of theft being carried out by employees it may be necessary to implement a search policy. Seek specific advice on the drafting and introduction of the policy.

Computer access

It may be helpful to link any required restrictions on access to computers and/or computer departments to the access procedure. The Computer Misuse Act 1990 makes an offence of:

(a) unauthorised access to computer material (i.e. both hacking and access by unauthorised users).

(b) unauthorised modification of computer material (e.g. the insertion of a data destruction devices – or 'time bombs' – such as the 'Friday 13th' or 'March 6th/Leonardo' programs).

(c) ulterior intent (i.e. unauthorised access for the purpose of committing a crime).

Penalties for unauthorised access (apart from those provided for under the Act which can be as much as five years' imprisonment and/or an unlimited fine) may include dismissal for employees. To ensure that any such dismissal is treated as being fair, organisations should make it clear to their employees that unauthorised use of or access to the computer system carries severe penalties. One way would be to include this in employment contracts and staff handbooks.

A supplementary policy/procedure such as the following might be appropriate:

Internal access

(a) Employees may operate only within the areas of their own departmental operations and service areas. Access to other areas is restricted to authorised personnel only. Access to the systems of the organisation, particularly, but not exclusively, the computer systems, is reserved to authorised personnel only. Unauthorised access to, or in any way tampering with, any computer system or software, or computer installation (including but not restricted to the items in this rule) will be regarded as gross misconduct and will render the offender liable to dismissal and possible prosecution under the Computer Misuse Act 1990 even if no physical damage results.

(b) All computer records will be backed up daily (or more often if required) with back-up records stored in (a remote location).

(c) Data files altered during daily working will also be backed up each day. Such back-up records will be stored in (a remote location).

(d) In no instance should any computer owned or leased by the business be used for playing games or for any purpose other than the legitimate work of the business. Nor shall employees using their own laptops, notebooks or other computers or electronic equipment use them for such purposes whilst at work. Nor may employees access the Internet (or any other information service obtained via computer access) whilst at work other than with the previous written permission of a director.

Any employee breaking these rules will be regarded as having committed serious industrial misconduct, the maximum penalty for which under the organisation's disciplinary policy is instant dismissal.

WARNING Not only can allowing access to the Internet consume considerable amounts of employees' time for questionable benefit, but also the connection of the internal system to an external provider lends itself to the penetration of the computer system by hackers. It is estimated that one computer system is broken into every 20 seconds.

(e) Whilst an internal system can be used for E-mail, care should be taken in such transmissions to avoid commenting on any individual or organisation.

WARNING Concern is growing at the casual use of such systems to make personal comments which may amount to slander or libel. Currently legislation is anticipated regarding the use of such systems.

(f) No software and/or disks, etc. other than those owned or leased by the business must be used in the business computers. All software and disks must be purchased new from recognised and reputable suppliers, backed by a confirmation that all such items are free from viruses, etc., and/or with a guarantee/liability acceptance that, in the event that virus(es) which have caused damage were present on purchase, the supplier will reimburse losses. Disks obtained via third parties may only be accessed after each has been checked for viruses and the consent of [a board director] has been obtained.

(g) Anti-virus programs should be used regularly (specify intervals) to check that all systems, software and disks, etc. (including back-up files) are virus-free. Any item found infected must be immediately separated from any networking arrangement, and steps taken to eliminate the virus.

2. Owners

Shareholders in limited companies, whether private limited companies or public limited companies (PLCs), have a number of rights of access in order to allow them to inspect certain statutory records of the company. The records they have a right to inspect are listed below.

Register of Members
Overseas Branch Register
Minutes of general meetings
Register of Directors and Secretary
Register of Directors' Shareholdings
Register of Significant Shareholdings
Directors' service contracts
Register of transactions not disclosed in the accounts under Companies Act 1985 section 330
Register of Disclosure of holders under section 212 of the Companies Act 1985
Register of Charges
Register of Debenture Holders

These records must generally be made available for a minimum of 2 hours each working day. A procedure such as that devised for employees access might usefully be drawn up so that such visitors are treated courteously and efficiently (see *ONE STOP Company Secretary*).

3. Public and creditors

The following registers (which must be provided for access by shareholders) must also be made available to members of the public.

Register of Members
Overseas Branch Register
Register of Directors and Secretary
Register of Directors' Shareholdings
Register of Significant Shareholdings
Register of Disclosure of holders under section 212 of the Companies Act 1985
Register of Charges

Again it may be helpful to draw up a procedure to ensure such requests are dealt with efficiently.

4. Official visitors

There are a large number of official (state) organisations, whose representatives have rights of access to the premises for the purpose of inspecting records and checking compliance with laws. In addition further organisations may have similar rights derived from contractual relationships (e.g. a lease of the premises and/or membership of a trade or similar organisation and so on).

The principal bodies having such rights are set out below. It may be helpful to brief receptionists on the manner of dealing with such persons.

Government and statutory regulatory agencies:

These include the Department of Trade and Industry (DTI), self-regulatory organisations (SRO), the Serious Fraud Office (SFO) and European Union competition law inspectors (EU).

Scope

The DTI has power to investigate company affairs, ownership, dealings in shares, including insider dealing. The exact nature of the investigation must be ascertained.

SROs have powers under the Financial Services Act to investigate the affairs of their members.

The SFO has powers, wider in many cases than those available to the police or SROs, to investigate matters of fraud likely to total in excess of £2 million and to be of public concern.

EU inspectors have rights (without notice) to enter the premises of organisations of member states under EU competition law, although it has been stated that in doing so they should try to act in accordance with the laws of the member state (and in concert with the domestic regulatory agency) concerned.

> *Note* The Office of Fair Trading has an obligation to investigate whether supplies of goods or services breach the principles of the Fair Trading Act 1973, i.e. whether control of a market is such that a reference should be made to the Mergers and Monopolies Commission, and the Competition Act 1980. It has no right of access although this is currently being sought.

Statutory reporting agencies

These include the Inland Revenue (IR), the Contributions Agency (CA) of the Department of Social Security (DSS), Customs and Excise (C&E), the Wages Councils (WC), rating authorities (RA), and the Occupational Pensions Authority (OPA).

IR powers of access tend to be exercised by the Audit Department of their Compliance unit, which has the duty of checking the validity of the way an employer has paid and deducted tax from employees.

The CA and the DSS have similar powers to the Inland Revenue.

C&E have wide powers of access in respect of their VAT collection duties.

WC (only for those employees whose occupations are covered by the remaining Wages Councils) officials have a right of access to check the display of the current Wages Council edict and to ensure payments, etc., are being made in accordance with it.

RAs have a right of access for the purpose of checking the valuation for the purposes of the Uniform Business Rate (or any appeal in respect thereof).

OPA have a right of access to check compliance with the requirements of the Pensions Act 1995.

Emergency and utility services

These include the fire, police, Health and Safety Executive, Environment Agency, and factory inspectorates, and gas, water and electricity utilities.

The fire service has the right of access to premises mainly for the purposes of checking compliance with the provision of fire certificates, and requirements regarding fire safety made by fire officer.

The police have no immediate right of access to premises other than with the permission of the owner unless in the belief, or officers are in connection with such belief, that a crime is about to, or is being committed, or in hot pursuit of a suspected person.

The Health and Safety Executive, environmental health officers, and factory inspectors have a range of powers which vary from industry to industry. Operators of large (and potentially hazardous) facilities are obliged (under the Control of Industrial Major Accident Regulations 1988) to file and keep up to date details of plans and emergency evacuations, etc. This will require an interview with the appropriate department which may well wish to check the site.

Utilities have rights of access to read meters and, if leaks/breaks are suspected, to rectify on an emergency basis which could entail forced entry.

Others

These may include the following:

The Department of Transport – may access the property to inspect transport operators licence and administration.

Local authorities have an increasing range of obligations, particularly under the Food Safety and Environment Protection Acts.

Trading Standards Officers need access to check details of the establishment to ensure compliance with the relevant trading law.

Landlord and agents may require access to inspect the condition and use of premises, assess value for insurance, prepare dilapidations reports, under the provisions of the lease and/or licence.

5. Trespassers

Whilst not on site by invitation, occupiers and/or owners have obligations under the OCCUPIER'S LIABILITY Acts to trespassers and particularly for the safety of children and others even though they are unlawfully on the premises.

> *Note*   In the case of *Margereson & Hancock v J W Roberts Ltd, the company was held to be liable to the widow of a man who had contracted a disease as a result of him playing, when a child, in the asbestos-ridden dust of their loading bay – where he had no right to be. Property occupiers need to be proactive to ensure trespassers' safety is maximised and their own liability is minimised.*

Acquisition – Financial

Introduction

The acquisition of any property, be it ownership or occupation under lease or licence, entails a commitment of resources. The question of whether it is appropriate for an organisation to commit such resources needs to be posed to those making such a decision. To aid the decision-making process all the salient expense factors need to be identified and quantified so that decisions can be made with the benefit of the facts. However, experience indicates that organisations often decide to invest in property without a full appreciation of the financial implications of such a decision.

Investigation

The following forms may be useful in identifying most of the major areas of expense. If such expense can be related (as the forms attempt to do) to the benefit likely to be derived from the investment then a proper cost – benefit evaluation can be arrived at.

> *Note* *These forms are suggested as examples only and need to be customised to suit the particular requirements of individual organisations. The forms assume that the organisation prepares a long-term financial/sales plan and commences with the requirement for individual parts of the organisation to determine the space they require for at least the duration of such a plan. From an analysis of future requirements the organisation can put together a 'premises requirement' and work towards the provision of suitable areas as they are required.*

ONE STOP PROPERTY

1. Forward planning form

Organisation .... Planning period 19.. – 20.. Department ....

	Current Space Usage	Annual Charges	Current Earnings
Income-generating	....	....	....
Ancillary	....	....	....
Storage	....	....	....
Display/reception	....	....	....
TOTAL	_____	_____	_____

Space required	19xx		19xx	
	Annual costs	Projected earnings	Annual costs	Projected earnings
Income-generating	....	....	....	....
Ancillary	....	....	....	....
Storage	....	....	....	....
Display/reception	....	....	....	....
TOTAL	_____	_____	_____	_____

Reasons for increase(s) _____

Space likely to be released from current allocation _____

	19xx		19xx	
	Annual costs	Projected income	Annual costs	Projected income
Income-generating	....	....	....	....
Ancillary	....	....	....	....
Storage	....	....	....	....
Display/reception	....	....	....	....
TOTAL	_____	_____	_____	_____

Reasons for decrease(s) _____

ACQUISITION — FINANCIAL

Notes to Form 1

(a) The form should be geared to fit the span of time covered by the plan. Space could be indicated in square feet or square metres.

(b) Calculating the costs as a proportion of the area occupied per department (no matter how crude – provided the same parameters are used for all) can aid the planning process itself.

(c) The split of type of space has been provided as a guide. Approaches will differ regarding the desirability or practicality or otherwise of this.

(d) Depending on the sophistication of the planning process, the annual charges could include (an appropriate proportion of) – rent (or INTERNAL RENT) rates, maintenance, decoration, heating, lighting, security and so on.

(e) Providing some kind of 'income' for each part of the facility against which the charges can be compared can assist in the general planning process as well as the facility planning.

(f) Any indication that additional space will be required should be required to be substantiated. Such a development should already have been addressed, of course, during the main planning process and thus can be cross-referenced.

(g) Space that is surplus to requirements can be identified in the same way as additional needs. Provided the space is freehold, or leasehold where there is permission to sublet, the possibility of using this space to generate income should be examined.

---

2. Acquisition justification form – freehold

Organisation .... Freehold Acquisition Assessment
Property address ....
Purpose ....

A. Rationale
Is acquisition in plan? YES/NO*
If NO, provide complete rationale and explain effect on plan.
....

If YES, is timing in accordance with plan? YES/NO*
If not provide explanation ....
....

B. Cost

Purchase price	£	
Purchase costs	£	(agents, surveyors, solicitors)
Fitting-out costs	£ _____	(confirmed estimate)
Total acquisition costs	£ _____	
Estimated annual charge	£	

C. Location

Explain rationale for selecting this site ....
What is planning authority designated use for the area? ....
What are prospects for disposal in long term?..
Any capital growth anticipated? YES/NO
If YES, explain type of growth/period, etc. ....

D. Usage

Is whole property to be used? YES/NO
If YES, state annual income from property ....
If NO, explain approach regarding surplus ....
Expected income from subletting, etc. ....

E. Running costs

Annual operating costs ....

(Provide analysis for duration of plan span of [specify])

> *Note* This could include the 'annual charge' (see B above), internal rent, cost of loan or depreciation, statutory imposition reserve, etc.

F. Alternative rationale

(That is, provide an explanation of how the situation will be addressed if this purchase is not proceeded with?)

Notes to form 2

(a) Unless the proposal has been previously addressed within the planning process the whole rationale needs to be examined.

(b) The means by which the operating department/unit, etc. is charged for the occupation needs to be determined either by means of a proportion of the original cost price, or by internal rent, depreciation charge, etc.

(c) The question of ultimate use or disposal should at least be addressed

(d) The concept of a statutory imposition reserve addresses the fact that increasingly commercial occupiers of property are required under legislation to carry out alterations, etc., to property where employees work and it would be prudent to allow some reserve for this.

ACQUISITION – FINANCIAL

3. Acquisition justification form – leasehold

Organisation ....   Leasehold Acquisition Assessment
Property address ....
Purpose ....

A. Commitment rationale
Is commitment in plan? YES/NO*
If NO, provide complete rationale and explain effect on plan ....
If YES, is timing in accordance with plan? YES/NO*
If NO, provide an explanation ....

B. Total expenditure commitment
Expenditure – multiply commencing annual rent
plus service charge (if any) by term of lease
or term to option date (if any).   £
Projected additional rent and service charge
    from reviews.   £
Total commitment (i.e. figure to be justified)   _____

                                                                                                       _____

What alternatives are there to the commitment to this lease? ....
....
Can lease term be shortened and is this appropriate? ....
If NO, can an option to break be introduced? ....
Possibilities of assignment (i.e. is lease marketable)? ....
Any possibility of acquiring freehold? YES/NO
If YES, what price? ....

C. Annual running costs
(Total annual expenditure including rent, rates, heating,
lighting, statutory imposition reserve, maintenance,
redecoration, dilapidation reserve) ....

D. Usage
Is whole property to be used? YES/NO
If NO, can surplus be sublet? YES/NO
If YES what is expected income to offset annual costs?..............................
If NO, explain rationale re surplus..

Notes to form 3

(a) The requirement for prospective occupiers to state alternatives should approval for occupation not be granted is used widely in the USA. Such alternatives could, for example, include:
i) a bought in service
ii) short term licensing
iii) outworking.

(b) The requirement to consider the implications of commitment to a long-term lease is mainly to underline that very point, i.e. it is a long-term commitment and any method of achieving flexibility should be considered.

(c) See the notes to the freehold acquisition form (form 2) for other guidance to the questions above.

Acquisition – General

Introduction

In acquiring the rights to property occupation, other than in a short-term licence, an organisation usually enters into a long-term commitment. The implications of such a commitment and all its obligations should be considered carefully, although experience indicates that this is not always the case. If these obligations are not appreciated, their effects can come as an expensive surprise to the unwary. The aspects and implications of the various types of occupation – FREEHOLD, LEASEHOLD and LICENCE–should be referred to. Whilst the choice between the various types of occupation may be predominantly a financial one (see ACQUISITION – FINANCIAL), there are a number of other considerations which need to be borne in mind. These considerations are referred to below, although more detailed guidance may be found in individual sections.

In addition, a number of considerations and implications also arise in considering acquisition – type of property, possibility of resale, type of location and any available assistance, cost of expenses related to the investment, etc.

Pre-commitment checklist

1. Location

Although it is rare for an ideal location to be found, one as near the ideal as possible should be sought (see RELOCATION – GENERAL AND PERSONNEL IMPLICATIONS). Recognition of this should generate the compilation of factors comprising an 'ideal' site. Where finance is a constraint there are a number of initiatives operated both by the state (DTI Enterprise Initiative, Urban Regeneration), by local authorities (Enterprise Zones) and by the European Union which aim at assisting occupiers financially who are ready to move to certain areas where employment is required. (The Department of the Environment has issued over 20 guides giving information about development policies in various areas. Expert advice should be sought if the organisation decides to try to obtain such assistance.)

2. Area

Before making a decision, the long-term future of the area should be considered. Is it likely that, should the organisation wish to dispose of the premises in the medium future, there will be a market for such premises in such a location? If not disposal may be costly. The position regarding Registration of Land on which the building stands should be investigated. Although an increasing proportion of land in the UK is now registered (i.e. details of position, history, ownership, restrictive covenants, etc., are on record with the Land Registry and allocated a Title Number) sizable areas (including much of London) are not yet registered which may make the investigation of title more difficult.

3. Type of property

Whilst a property that fits the exact requirements of the organisation is ideal, if such requirements are very unusual, it may be difficult to dispose of the property in the future. Some organisations feel that acquiring a listed building may add to their image, only to find that there are severe restrictions regarding use and alteration of such a property.

4. Pre-acquisition survey

Whether the property is to be purchased or leased, a full structural survey should be commissioned. Despite the expense involved, which may, given the current somewhat depressed state of the commercial property market, be open to negotiation, failure to establish the true state of the property could prove costly in the long term. This is especially the case with property subject to a full repairing lease. Under the terms of such a lease the Landlord will have the immediate right to require the lessee to rectify repairs, etc., and if the clause reads 'put and keep repaired' the obligation exists to bring the property to a fair state of repair no matter how dilapidated it may have been initially. Establishing the state of the building at least enables the purchaser to take a commercial decision in recognition of such potential obligations. Indeed the existence of a professionally compiled survey may be a valuable negotiating factor in arriving at the determination of price, rent and/or premium.

5. Inherent defects.

Another advantage of the survey is that it may disclose any inherent defects in the building which, through negotiation, may be taken out of any commitment as far as rectification and/or repair.

6. Condition of schedule

Such a schedule may also be negotiated to minimise onerous repair/rectification obligations when entering into a lease. An agreed schedule can have the effect of minimising the lessee's obligations to repair to the state demonstrated by the schedule itself.

7. Covenants

The full effect of all the covenants required to be included in the lease should be explained to those who will actually operate from the building in case any (such as restrictive opening hours) would inhibit full use of the building.

> **WARNING** Whereas legal advisers may well indicate (an) onerous covenant(s), they may not always be aware of the practical implications of such covenants on the operation of the business. Someone aware of such practical requirements should review ALL covenants and their effect before commitment.

8. Privity of contract

If privity of contract requirements or their equivalent are included in the lease, the lease should contain permission for the lessee to sub or underlet as an option to assignment. In this way, should the premises become surplus to requirements, and an alternative occupier be found, the lessee can sublet or UNDERLET (rather than ASSIGN), knowing that should the new occupier fail, the organisation retains rights (lost in the event of assignment) to re-occupy and/or to re-let.

9. Planning application

Any restrictions placed on occupation by planning consents and/or conditions, and/or covenants contained in the Conveyance need to be fully appreciated (and costed).

10. Acquisition costs

As well as the actual purchase price all solicitors' and agents' costs, stamp duty, insurance (cover should be arranged from exchange of contracts), etc. should be estimated and included in the budget. Some organisations require the total costs to be justified as part of the acquisition approval. For leasehold premises justification may be required of the total rental exposure for the term of the lease (ignoring or including reviews) since this is the commitment being entered into.

11. Occupation costs

The full costs of occupying and running the facility need to be assessed (and may need to be justified). Where relocation is taking place, the current costs of heating and lighting may be capable of being extrapolated (to take account of a building of different size and/or configuration). If an existing building is being acquired, enquiry of the previous occupier may also provide a guide to these costs. Obviously the effect of building's costs as well as cost of money invested, depreciation, etc., needs to be taken into account. The aim should be to have a comprehensive budget recognising all expenditure in advance.

> *Note* *If the use of the building – or its configuration in terms of occupation – is to be changed, the question of the RATING valuation – and any appeal – should be considered.*

12. Access

Access to the premises, car parking and relationships with NEIGHBOURS should be investigated

13. Personnel

Staffing and employees' travelling conditions may need consideration.

Commitment checklist

1. Customising

Rarely will any building be ideal for immediate occupation and most will require some customising. All such works will need to be approved under BUILDING REGULATIONS and be subject to the requirements issued by the Fire Officer to comply with the issue of a FIRE CERTIFICATE. Where the occupation is leasehold, the approval of the landlord must also be sought prior to any works being effected carried out.

2. Works approval

Landlord's approval can be obtained either formally (under a licence to carry out works) or sometimes informally (by the landlord signing copies of the plans and specification setting out the work to be conducted). Usually the formal route is necessary which will not only require a deed to be drawn up, at the lessee's expense, but will also set out conditions regarding the works and normally an obligation on the lessee as to REINSTATEMENT before the termination of the lease. The triple cost effect of such works should not be overlooked. The lessee will need to pay for the works to be completed, then for them to be removed when the lease terminates, at which time, since the premises must be left in a good state of repair, they may also be involved in substantial making good.

3. Funding the works

Responsibility for funding payment for the works must be established. Such costs can be met by either party. If the landlord pays, it may be agreed that the costs can be recoverable by the rent being increased or by payment of an additional sum at the same time as rent is paid. Although this makes the relationship somewhat 'tidier' since the lessee is simply occupying a facility the entire cost of which has been met by the landlord, if the rent itself is increased it may have repercussions at times of RENT REVIEW in terms of the relationship of the rent paid by tenants in similar properties in the immediate area. The 'rentalised' costs may be better dealt with as a charge entirely separate to the rent (even if collected at the same time).

If the lessee funds the works, then not only should the triple cost effect be borne in mind but also it should be agreed that the effect of the works should be ignored at the time of the first RENT REVIEW – and ideally at the time of all rent reviews although this is a matter for negotiation. If this is not stipulated, then the lessee could, having paid for works which increase the value of the premises, be asked to pay a rent partly enhanced by the works themselves. If the landlord resists this 'ignore the effect of the works at rent review' argument and requires the full value to be reflected at review either the landlord should fund the works, or some dilution of other covenants (e.g. repairing and/or reinstatement obligations) should be negotiated.

4. Accountability

Ideally, completion of the acquisition phase should take place in sufficient time for any customised works and any setting-up work to take place before any move or physical occupation. Rarely does this occur and usually there needs to be some compromise – often with employees trying to set up and commence working whilst builders are still finishing off. This is far from ideal if only for the question of responsibility. Usually the terms of a building contract will require the contracting builder to take responsibility for the property during the works (and to effect insurance related to this). If staff from the employing organisation occupy the premises before the builder has 'handed over', responsibility, in the event of any loss or damage, may be blurred. In addition, the builder may be able to refute any attempt to enforce any penalties for late completion by claiming that his staff were being 'hampered' by the occupation.

> Note: The moment any part of the building is occupied for use RATES may be payable on the whole.

Advertising Hoardings

Introduction

Commercial properties with large external walls with few windows have a space which may lend itself to the erection of advertising hoardings as a source of income.

Permission

Assuming the owner of the building is agreeable to the installation of such a hoarding, permission will be required from the local planning office. The installation also raises questions of public liability. For these reasons it may be advisable for the owner to delegate to a specialist company all that is required to gain permission as well as to install, maintain and insure the hoarding. A legal agreement should be drawn up which should include the requirement that at the end of the term, the other party will be responsible for removing the hoarding and making good the wall and that in the meantime they will be responsible for all and any works required to be done to erect the hoarding (including obtaining and renewing planning permission) and for the maintenance of the hoarding and the wall to which it is fixed thereafter.

Fee

In return for granting permission to install and keep the hoarding the organisation should negotiate an annual fee which could, depending upon the position, amount to several hundred pounds. The term of the agreement should be kept to five or seven years. Advertising agreements tend not to have review clauses and keeping the term relatively short should allow the income to be renegotiated on expiry.

Early removal

To allow the owner to develop or alter the premises, the agreement should incorporate a clause allowing termination for these purposes by the owner on, say, six months' notice.

Archiving

Introduction

Control of property assets cannot be effected properly without information, which needs to be instantly available to the property administrator. The sourcing and collation of data that leads to the compilation of a PROPERTY REGISTER is essential. However the source material for such information is often original documentation which may have a value in its own right (e.g. inconvenience should it be lost) and thus requires adequate protection.

Freehold data

Transfer of freehold property is usually effected by means of a conveyance which is a document of title. Since 1937, land has been required to be registered with the Land Registry on sale. Nevertheless, around a third of all UK properties (including most of the properties in London) are unregistered. For registered property therefore the Land Registry will have details of ownership. However, the loss of a conveyance can cause considerable inconvenience and cost in proving title on disposal. Fortunately, a conveyance is seldom the only deed relating to a property and on each successive transfer of ownership the bundle of documents evidencing title grows. All such documents – easements, rights of access, consents, etc. – need protection.

In addition evidence of all alterations to the property – approvals, plans, specifications, etc. – should be preserved with the title deeds, as should all updates of such information.

An index or schedule of the items should be prepared and copies kept both with the deeds and by the Property administrator.

WARNING Strict control over the protection of title needs to be effected since in any audit of the financial records of the organisation in which reference is made to the value of its properties, the auditors may wish to see evidence of ownership. Some form of control register such as is set out below may be advisable to act as a document of record concerning to whom deeds, etc., were lent and when. In passing title deeds outside the immediate control of the Property administrator a receipt for the entire schedule of documents loaned should be obtained and the receipt kept with the register. On return the items should be checked against the schedule and a counter receipt issued. Note that the second schedule may contain items additional to the original (or there may have been authorised deletions). The revised schedule should become the new record to be kept with the documents and by the Property administrator.

Date	Property	Deeds	Schedule reference	Reason withdrawn	Sent to	Returned

Leasehold data

A lease is not a document of title, it merely conveys a right of occupation on the lessee. As such, however, it should be preserved safely. In certain cases leases may well have a financial value to the lessee and the points referred to above in relation to the audit should not be overlooked. Similarly, all documentation relating to the occupation (plans, specifications, approvals, etc.) as well as any deeds of variation, rent review confirmations, etc., should be preserved. Where the landlord has granted approval to the tenant to carry out alterations by signing and returning plans (rather than insisting on a Deed or licence evidencing the works) such plans should be preserved as a variation of the lease.

System

To ensure that all records (including those not related to property) are properly stored, a suitable policy and procedure such as the following should be adopted.

Document and records preservation policy [Organisation]

(a) Responsibility for preserving the various books, registers and records of the company, in order to comply with legislation and business practice, is devolved to (Company Secretary).

(b) Such responsibility will include:

(i) ensuring safe storage with reasonable accessibility whilst the items are current.

(ii) provision of adequate back-up systems capable of providing current record data, should the original be lost for any reason.

(iii) archiving records in accordance with a procedure and timetable to be devised.

(iv) ensuring preservation of such records in those archives.

(c) The various terms of retention as set out in the Institute of Chartered Secretaries handbook on the subject, or Tolley's *Business Administration* [or similar reference material] (subject to any extension, but not contraction, of the suggested time limits for reasons particular to the organisation) are to be adhered to at all times.

(d) Suitably secure premises/facilities will be utilised for this purpose. Such premises, etc., will need to provide protection from rodents, fire, flood, intruders, etc.

(e) The [Company Secretary or equivalent executive] will be required to report annually on compliance with the requirements of this procedure.

Protection

All the deeds and documents referred to above require protection. In some cases they may need to be deposited with (for example) the bankers of the organisation should they be used as security for loans. On making such a deposit, those receiving the items should be asked to confirm that they will hold them securely, store them safely (in fireproof cabinets) and deliver them up when the loan is repaid.

Other than when out on loan or held by third parties (e.g. solicitors) pending sale, etc., the items should be stored internally in fireproof cabinets or safes. Wherever possible such cabinets should be stored on the ground floor or basement. If the cabinet is stored on an upper storey, there is a danger in a fire, that even though the cabinet can resist a fire, it may burst open should it fall through collapsed floors. This danger can be minimised by using cabinets claimed to be burst-proof. In the aftermath of the terrorist campaign of the late 1980s and early 1990s, many organisations began creating bomb-proof rooms within their facilities. Whilst there will no doubt be considerable pressure on the space available in such rooms, consideration should be given to using part of such a room for the protection of deeds and documents related to property matters.

> <u>Note</u> *If protection is provided by means of a room, checks should be made to ensure that not only is the room bomb-, fire- and water-proof but also that it is rodent- and insect-proof.*

Copies

Both for instant access and also for recovery of data in the event of a loss of the originals it may be prudent to microfilm or otherwise record copies of the original deeds, etc. Reference should be made to British Standards to ensure proper steps are taken when copying the records. For microfilming the standard is BS6498 whilst for information stored on electronic document management systems the reference is PD0008. Subject to proof of reliability the Civil Evidence Act 1995 permits documents to be retained on computer (including records stored on compact disks to be used as evidence).

Assignment

> **Introduction**
>
> Selling or conveying a freehold property is relatively straight-forward since the ownership (and thus control) of the property rests with the vendor (seller). However, selling (assigning) the interest that the lessee has in a lease is always subject to the interest of the landlord (and any superior landlord(s)).

Preparation

Preparation for assignment should begin during the negotiations for the lease. In other words, in contemplating entering into a long-term commitment, the possibility of wishing to cease such occupation prior to the termination of the lease must also be considered. Therefore, it becomes necessary to try to reserve to the lessee the right to assign their interest. The landlord will normally wish, if not to deny such a right, at least to ensure that any assignment can be made only with their prior written permission and with some control over the proposed assignees (that is their new tenants). It is normal for lease clauses to stipulate:

(a) that the original lessee cannot assign part only of the property leased by them.

(b) that the lessee can assign only with the prior written agreement of the landlord.

Since such a wording may be regarded as unduly restrictive it is normal for the lessee to add to the wording a provision requiring landlord's consent 'such agreement not to be unreasonably withheld'. This proviso softens the strictness of the original clause although it must be said that the only way to prove that agreement was being unreasonably withheld may be to go to the court. Obviously the threat of taking the matter that far may help force a recalcitrant landlord to agree the assignment.

Compliance with covenants

Inherent in every lease is the requirement on both parties to comply with the COVENANTS contained therein. Most of the usual covenants are ongoing, requiring constant attention for the whole term of the lease. Failure to comply is a breach of the lease and could thus form the basis for an action by one party against the other. Normally this will result in the landlord taking action against the lessee but occasionally it works in the other direction. Thus in the case of *British Telecom v Sun Life Assurance* the Court held that a landlord was obliged to keep parts of a property not occupied by the lessee in good repair at all times (i.e. it could not have a 'reasonable time' in which to carry them out but needed to carry out such repairs immediately).

Thus in seeking the landlord's permission to sell or assign their interest in the lease, the lessee needs to ensure that they have complied with all covenants since failure to comply may be used by the landlord as a reason for not granting permission to the assignment.

Application

Assuming that covenants have been or are agreed to be complied with, and a new tenant has been found by the lessee, application for assignment can be made to the landlord. Understandably, the landlord will wish to ensure that the proposed lessee is at least of similar financial standing and probity to the existing lessee. They will normally insist on references being provided and should there be any question concerning the proposed lessee's capacity to comply with the requirements of the lease, guarantees may also be sought. Whilst this may be regarded as an irritant by the existing lessee, it is in fact a protection for them just as much as for the landlord. Under the PRIVITY OF CONTRACT rule, for all leases entered into prior to 1 January 1996, the original lessee of a lease is ultimately responsible for any non-compliance with covenants (including payment of outgoings, rent, etc.) of an assignee. The problem is that although the original lessee has a degree of control over the person/organisation to whom they assign, they seldom have such control over subsequent assignments. One way in which this can be overcome is by inserting a clause in the deed of assignment requiring the assignee to gain the original lessee's approval to any further assignment (and for any further assignees similarly to gain such approval) although it has to be said that this may be both resisted and, even if agreed, difficult to enforce.

Grant

The landlord may request additional information (e.g. requesting to see copies of the financial records for the assignee for the last two or more years, etc.) before agreeing in principle to the proposal. Having agreed, a deed of assignment will need to be drawn up and signed (or sealed) by all three parties (landlord, lessee and assignee). The costs of such a deed, as well as the costs of granting approval, will normally be levied on the lessee or the assignee.

Protection

The problem for the original lessee when assigning a lease is that in passing over the responsibilities under the lease to the assignee, the original lessee also passes over the right to occupy. Should the assignee fail, although the responsibility for the financial obligations under the lease reverts to the lessee, the right to occupy does not, it may therefore be prudent to try to:

(a) insert a clause whereby the landlord undertakes to notify the lessee immediately an assignee fails to pay rent, etc., so that the lessee is aware of its potential liability. In such an event the lessee may be able to take steps to try to minimise the exposure, for example by approaching the current tenant direct.

(b) to try to obtain the right of re-entry to the premises in the event of an assignee failing.

Following the collapse of retail sales in the early 1990s and the parallel collapse in the retail property market, a number of retailers who had assigned leases when the economy was buoyant were faced with large bills following the failures of assignees. There were two widespread complaints:

(a) that landlords had waited too long before taking action and thus had allowed their debts to mount,

(b) that had they had the right of re-entry, the lessee could have re-opened the shop and traded there themselves. Whilst they may not have made money, equally they would not have had a large bill for arrears of rent, etc.

Advice

Assignment of a lease is a complicated and potentially expensive process. To ensure as much protection as possible specific legal advice should be taken.

Building Regulations

Introduction

All work whether erection of new or alterations to existing buildings (except relatively minor works and works subject to a number of exceptions in Schedule 2 of the Building Regulations 1991 (SI 1991 2768) amended by the Building (Amendment) Regulations 1994 (SI 1994 1850)) will usually require approval under building regulations. Since approval is linked to the requirements under fire certification, an application in respect of most buildings being used for commercial purposes will also require clearance under fire precautions legislation. The Building Regulations together with advice regarding their application which is listed in approved documents, emanates from the Building Act 1984.

WARNING It should be noted that even the erection of a 'de-mountable' partition may, should it create an office within an office, infringe fire regulations. A full investigation of the effect of even such minor works should be carried out and advice sought.

Preparation

Obtaining approval under building regulations may be time-consuming particularly if the original suggestions are not agreed or are agreed subject to alterations. The compiling and submission of building plans for approval should be handled by an appropriately qualified person who, by virtue of experience and local contacts may be able to save time (and money) by ensuring that proposals which will not meet approval are not put forward. Informal contact with the appropriate officials, either by a qualified surveyor or similar, or even the property occupier, may save time.

Administration

The administration of the building regulations requirements is effected by local authorities. To commence obtaining clearance, those wishing to carry out building works must deposit full plans of the works contemplated. It is prudent to ensure the timetable allows for the time that will be taken by the local authority considering the proposals. Whilst it may be possible to start some works in advance of clearance, there is a risk that any work which does not comply with the regulations or requirements may have to be rectified.

Appeal

Should a local authority reject their plans, an applicant has a right of appeal to the Department of the Environment. Whilst this may have some attraction, the time taken before a decision is forthcoming should not be underestimated.

Compliance

Should a person, required to submit plans under the building regulations, not submit them or should they contravene the regulations in some way they are liable to a fine of up to £5,000 plus a daily fine of £50 for the duration of the default. The local authority can also require the person responsible to demolish any building erected without regulations approval and/or carry out alterations as required to make the building comply with the regulations. Should the owner not comply within 28 days the authority has the right to enter the land, carry out the required works and recover all costs incurred from the person responsible.

Definitions

Building works for the purposes of building regulations are defined as:

(a) erection/extension or material alteration.

(b) provision or material alteration of a controlled service (i.e. toilet, drainage, water, etc. provisions).

(c) change of use and work in connection with a change of use.

(d) underpinning and wall insulation work.

> Note   This is an outline only, the purpose of which is to demonstrate the widespread application of the regulations and the need to gain clearance of non-application or permission prior to ANY work taking place. For detailed guidance specific advice should be sought and reference should be made to the regulations themselves.

Building Works

> **Introduction**
>
> The requirement to gain official approval/clearance for building works is considered in BUILDING REGULATIONS. The subject of this section is the control of building works themselves assuming all necessary approvals have been obtained (not least from the owner of the property if leased – see COVENANTS and ACQUISITION).

Documentation

No matter how small are the works contemplated, a contract should be drawn up. Whilst for minor works this may seem unnecessary, it should not be overlooked that the damage that could be done to a building (and the business being carried on from it) during building works can be immense. It is not unknown for millions of pounds of damage to be caused as a result of action (or inaction) during relatively minor building work (e.g. the fire at Windsor Castle). Agreeing a contract enables both parties to stipulate what is required as well as setting out the responsibilities of each during the works. This is particularly important when the works are to be carried out whilst the building is being used for its main purpose.

Included in the contract should be:

(a) a detailed specification of the works (so that in the event of any dispute the parties have an agreed specification to refer to for determination).

(b) a detailed timetable and progress chart.

(c) a time/cost analysis with details of any bonus payments for early completion (or penalties for late completion).

(d) the names and title of all those involved in the works with their level of authority (see below).

(e) details of the third party to be used in the event of any dispute between the parties.

> <u>Note</u>   Increasingly, Alternative Dispute Resolution (ADR) is being used to determine disputes. Under this process both parties nominate a third

party to determine their dispute agreeing to pay 50% of the costs involved. This avoids the recourse for resolution of problems to the legal profession which tends to be costly in both money and time. A guidance booklet on ADR is available from local courts.

Safety

Works

Of paramount importance is the safety both of those carrying out the works and of those working within the building during the works. Under the Construction (Design and Management) Regulations 1994 which came into effect on 31 March 1995, for any building work which is to last longer than 30 days and involves more than four people or is to boiler/heating plant or is to be carried on inside offices or shops without interrupting normal activities, a safety planning supervisor must be appointed and a suitable health and safety plan must be compiled.

The plan itself must address various phases in the process:

(a) the tender period when details of health and safety requirements must be passed by the employer to those tendering for the work,

(b) the design period when the designer needs to consider health and safety requirements in planning the design and to advise the employer of these and their implications,

(c) the construction phase when health and safety becomes the responsibility of a planning supervisor who is required to coordinate and manage health and safety matters in liaison with the principal contractor.

A safety plan must be compiled, complied with at all times and made available to interested parties.

> **WARNING** The foregoing is a brief outline only of the Construction (Design and Management) Regulations 1994. For greater coverage, reference should be made to the Health and Safety Executive information sheets – Construction Sheets Nos. 38 – 44.

Premises

In many cases a contractor will be working on a client's premises whilst at least part of those premises are in ordinary use. It is important that the safety matters related to the works themselves (as covered above) are also brought to the attention of the contractor, employees, subcontractors and their employees and anyone else required to be present at the property. A copy of the Health and Safety policy and any other requirements should form part of the contract documentation and a clause in the contract should make it clear that the client expects adherence to the policy at all times.

Other requirements, such as those listed below should also be made clear:

(a) security rules to be observed,
(b) disconnection of electricity only to be made after a clear day's notice (to avoid having an impact on computerisation, etc.),
(c) builders to refrain from commenting audibly on any member of the client's staff – or any member of the public if work is going on outside the premises.

Increasingly clients are also inserting a requirement that should, for any reason, they not wish a member of the contractor's staff, or any subcontractor or their employee(s) to work on the contract then that person or organisation must be removed by the main contractor.

Control

Normally a contractor will assume responsibility for the area covered by the building works (that is the area set out in the specification). Other than those working on the project, official visitors and the contractor's staff, agents and suppliers, no-one else should be present without the permission of the contractor. Such a rule may need to be relaxed where work is being carried on within the working environment where the organisation is seeking to conduct normal business. The problem with shared access is that in the event of any loss or accident it may be difficult to allocate exact responsibility. Since the contractor will normally be required to effect insurance to cover the works and potential liabilities, there is a possibility of conflict between two or more insurers. The problem may be alleviated by the client insisting that the contractor uses the organisation's own buildings/contents insurer.

Variation

Few building contracts run to their completion without at least one variation of the original specification. Whilst some of these may be the result of unforeseen snags and be requested by the builder, most tend to emanate from the client and are the result of second (or more) thoughts. Second thoughts may be sound and logical – but they also tend to be expensive particularly if some of the original work has already been completed. There should be a strictly enforced rule that only one nominated client's representative is empowered to agree variations (this is one reason for inserting the names of relevant personnel in the contract). This means that unless the contractor has authority from that person the variation is unauthorised and, at least in theory, the contractor cannot charge for it.

Originally the contract should have specified within it both time and price for the agreed specification. Whilst most people will appreciate that changing the works means a variation of the price, they do not always realise that there may be corresponding effect on the time specified. If the contract stipulates that there is an agreed time (and particularly if there are damages linked to a failure to keep within such time), all variations should address the contract term as well as the costs. Thus each time there is a variation to the specification not only should it be authorised by the person so empowered (and only by such person) but also a price needs to be agreed and the effect on the contract period needs to be re-assessed. If this is not done at the time, the contractor, should the contract overrun, will be able to claim, with some justification, that the number of variations were directly responsible for the contract being late and thus the impact of damages for late completion is negated.

The following example of a contract variation form requires completion of both cost and time alteration boxes.

Completion

The building profession is notorious for poor finishing. For this reason all building contracts should stipulate:

(a) practical completion and handover is not to be made until snagging is completed.

(b) a [six month] defects liability period.

(c) [2.5 – 10%] retentions.

Snagging

Before the works are handed over to the client it is usual for the latter (or his agent, e.g. an architect) to tour the works listing (usually small) items that need finishing or remedial attention. Only when such works are attended to should practical completion be certified and the works handed over.

Defects liability period

This is usually a six month period during which problems with the works should be noted by the client so that at the end of the period the contractor can be presented with a list of items which need rectifiying.

BUILDING WORKS

Organisation Name ....   **Project** ....

Variation Order No ....

This order is made this .... day of .... 199........

and varies the term/amount* of order no .... placed

on .... (builder/supplier) on .... (date).

Details of alteration	**Value/Time**

1 .... £................

2 .... etc. £................

Total value addition/reduction £................
(as approved by Capital Expenditure form ref ....)

Total time addition/reduction in days ....

Authorised by .... (signature)

.... (position) .... (date)

Received by .... (builder/supplier)

.... (position) .... (date)

Copies to :   Builder/supplier

Architect/surveyor/building project manager

Finance department

(Others)

Note Alterations to the original contract may only be made following the issue of an authorised variation order, and to the extent of the amount of cost/saving/time as shown thereon.

WARNING If the works covered by such a variation order are substantial it may be necessary to reconsider the safety plan prepared previously in respect of the works for any implications and required revisions.

Retention

A retention is merely a deduction (of 2.5%, 5% or 10%) from the total contract sum which is held by the client as a form of guarantee or incentive that the contractor will complete the full specification and, if the client is unhappy with the finish, will return to complete it satisfactorily. If there is difficulty getting the contractor to return to carry out the works the retention sum is then available to pay other contractors to finish the works.

With a large contract where payments are made in stages as the work progresses, the percentage retention is usually made from each stage payment. It may be helpful to link the release of the retention, subject to all works being completed, to the end of the defects liability period, although if the client is generally satisfied with the standard of the works, part of the retention may be released before that date.

Subcontractors' retention

The contractor should be requested to deduct the contract rate of retention from payments made to any subcontractor, so that there is in turn an incentive for the subcontractor to return and complete/rectify.

Although the principle of the retention is sound, it is most effective in cases where the rate is 10% or more. Where the rate is 5% or less, the sum involved can be relatively so small that subcontractors can afford to ignore the 'incentive' offered to return and rectify particularly if this means they have to pull employees off current jobs generating funds to do so. They are often prepared to forgo the money to avoid the time involvement.

> **WARNING** Where there are subcontractors it may be advisable for the client to check from time to time that they are being paid by the main contractor. It is not unknown for unscrupulous builders to retain the contract monies paid on account, withholding sums due in respect of work satisfactorily completed by the subcontractors. Whilst the client has no liability to the subcontractors they can still become involved in the ensuing argument.

Inspection

Under the contract the contractor is normally required to rectify omissions and/or poor work at the end of the defects liability period. To check the works required the contractor will inspect the area of the works against the original specification and any variations. Before that inspection the employer should carry out their own inspection (also referring to the specification and variations) preparing a list of items to bring to the attention of the contractor.

Condition, Schedule of

Introduction

In acquiring property assets the occupier (whether it be on a freehold or leasehold basis) accepts considerable responsibilities for those assets on a long-term basis. It is sound business sense to ensure that, as far as possible, the state of the property (structure, repair, redecoration etc.) is known. However, this recommendation should be regarded as an absolute necessity when entering into a lease with extensive repairing and redecorating covenants which could be invoked to requiring the lessee to put the premises into a good state of repair. Where the survey discloses that the premises are not in a good state of repair, consideration should be given to taking the matter one stage further by converting an assessment of the state of the premises into a schedule evidencing the state to which, but not beyond which, the premises must be repaired/redecorated – in short a schedule of the condition of the premises when responsibility was assumed.

Survey

A surveyor should be retained to inspect the whole property, to report on its state and to prepare a schedule showing the state in general and the areas where there needs to be work carried out in particular. In view of the potential liabilities and costs that could be incurred, any suggestion that the fee involved should be saved by waiving the need for a survey should be argued against as a false economy.

Agreeing the imposition

Generally landlords dislike schedules of condition as not only do they negate the concept of the lessee bearing responsibility for repair and redecoration (thus restricting this covenant) but also they have the effect of reducing the potential value of their investment since a leasehold property with a schedule of condition is a less attractive proposition than such a property where the lessee remains fully responsible for the state of the property. However it may be possible to obtain agreement to a schedule being written into the lease if, for example:

(a) the terms of trade are in favour of the purchaser (i.e. there is little demand for property).

(b) the prospective lessee is attractive to the landlord (e.g. they are regarded as reliable tenants) and the fact that they are the lessees may enhance the investment to an extent greater than the reduction occasioned by the imposition of a schedule of condition.

Compiling

Although a surveyor's written schedule may be sufficient to outline the condition of the premises as at the stated date, it may be preferable to record the state of the property partly by a written schedule but also partly either by photographs or, preferably, by video. The advantage of using a video is that the film can encompass a very wide area which could otherwise only be covered by hundreds of photos. Cross-referencing the video image to the written schedule can provide a comprehensive and accurate guide to the state of the premises. A camera which inserts the date on the film should be used so that the image on the film evidences the date of the record which itself should be at or around the commencement date of the lease and/or the commencement of the period during which the lessee accepts liability for the property. It is unlikely that the lessee will be able to prepare the schedule without some input from the landlord. It is more likely that the preparation of such a schedule will need to be done by, or at least under the control of the landlord or his agent.

Recording

Having prepared the schedule, a copy needs to be written into the lease or in some way referred to within the lease so that its existence and scope cannot be ignored or challenged later (when one or other or even both parties to the lease may have changed).

Waiving

Such a schedule is a protection for the lessee. However, it may be that the lessee would prefer the premises to be brought to a better condition. In this case there is no reason why such work should not be carried out – the schedule merely prevents the landlord from requiring work to be carried out which provides a better state of repair than that existing when the lessee took responsibility.

Buying out

The landlord's preference, particularly should they wish to sell their interest, is normally for the lease to be free of such a schedule. In such circumstances it may be possible to negotiate value in return for the schedule being removed from the lease – e.g. either a rent-free period or a cash sum.

Contaminated Land

Introduction

With greater attention being given to environmental matters, the question of the responsibility for and rectification of land contaminated as a result of commercial activities has assumed considerable importance and the thrust of legislation is increasingly to 'make the polluter pay' either by contributing to the cleansing of such land or by actually carrying out the cleansing. Anyone buying land or a business with land should obtain appropriate environmental warranties in the contract.

Background

Under the Environmental Protection Act 1990, local authorities were charged with the duty of setting up Registers of Contaminated Land. Details of land perceived to be contaminated would be entered in the registers and it was intended that, even if the land was subsequently 'cleansed', the land would remain listed (and presumably as a result of such listing would command a lower value than land not so listed).

In fact, these registers were not set up mainly because there was considerable concern that in recording details of such land at a time when the property market was suffering from a slump in demand would lead to widespread property blight.

Under the Environment Act 1995, the concept of contaminated land was readdressed in a somewhat diluted version of the original requirements.

The main points are listed below.

(a) Where there is contaminated land remedial action will be required where there is 'significant harm' or 'pollution of controlled waters' and there are cost-effective methods of cleansing.

(b) Local authorities will be required to identify land within their boundaries which is contaminated. Heavily contaminated land will be classified as 'special sites' requiring special provisions. Following a three month 'consultation period', the local authority can serve a remediation notice on the 'appropriate person'. If this notice is not complied with then the authority can enter the land and cleanse it, recovering the costs from the appropriate person. It can place a charge in its favour on the land if these costs are not reimbursed.

(c) the appropriate person is the person who caused the contamination. This may not be the owner although if the polluter cannot be found it may be the owner at the time who has to pay. However, a polluter who can be traced and who sells contaminated land at a reduced price has the possibility of a double loss – the fact that the price was reduced and the later requirement to cleanse.

It may be some time before the requirements under this Act are brought into effect and the detailed codes of practice required under the Act will need to be carefully studied. Those purchasing land which they believe may be contaminated may wish to consider trying to insert a guarantee into any sale and purchase agreement whereby they will be reimbursed by the vendor if required to cleanse the land. The alternative is to try to obtain insurance though cover is unlikely to be available at an economic price.

Contingency Planning

Introduction

Although a great deal of time is spent in planning for the future in terms of projecting sales, new products, etc., only a minority of organisations spend any time planning for their reactions should disaster (a major fire, explosion, building collapse, etc.) strike. Considering that there is usually plenty of time to correct shortfalls in sales, delivery date of new products, etc., and very little time when disaster strikes this is perhaps illogical.

Preparation

1. Identify a list of the occurrences which could affect the organisation severely.

2. Set out the names of personnel best placed to deal with each such occurrence.

3. Request each set of individuals to prepare an outline plan to cope with the disaster they have identified.

4. Review the plans at a senior level.

    Note Experience suggests that contemplation of disaster often generates ideas which can be incorporated into and improve current working practices. In fact, contingency planning is often incorporated into the planning process.

5. Review and update the plans each year (or more often if members of the teams and/or working practices change).

6. Generally prepare and update a list of telephone contacts (including own staff and professional advisers), particularly when business continues outside normal office hours and/or remote from administration/ responsible management.

7. Incorporate all plans into folders to be kept by each senior executive (with copies kept both at and away from the work location).

8. Specific aspects to be addressed by individual organisations if required include the following.

(a) If there is a public profile:

(i) identify and train a media spokesperson (not having someone available for comment is potentially dangerous).

(ii) set up a 24-hour telephone hotline.

(iii) make available skilled personnel to counsel and console those suffering from any trauma, and to deal patiently with those making enquiries regarding information, details of relatives, etc.

(b) If there is a need to source alternative production facilities:

(i) source list for all services identified as being needed.

(ii) record details of officials with whom the business may need to meet (e.g. at investigation and governmental agencies).

iii) source details (constantly updated) of all alternative sites for administration and/or production.

(c) In a small organisation with limited management resources:

(i) keep up to date management succession plans showing who could take over in an emergency.

(d) If involved in producing for consumers:

(i) devise recall and replacement/refund procedures for faulty or contaminated product and so on.

Example

Taking what is probably the most widely experienced disaster – that of fire – as an example, it is relatively easy to extend a simple fire evacuation procedure to form an important first step of a contingency or disaster plan.

1. Immediate action

(a) Sound alarm and evacuate.

(b) Check attendance register against evacuees.

(c) Advise firefighters of dangerous materials location.

(d) Shut off services.

(e) Provide information to neighbours, customers, media, etc.

CONTINGENCY PLANNING

2. Follow-up

(a) Postpone deliveries.

(b) Lay off staff (or find other work), retain key skills.

(c) Seek alternative premises (in accordance with requirements).

(d) Cover dislocation to production, etc., with identified temporary arrangements.

(e) Utilise back up services.

(f) Interface with media, industry body, trades unions, customers, suppliers, etc.

(g) Liaise with landlords, planners, architects, builders, etc.

Case study

Consideration of a particular problem may assist in explaining the type of approach that assists in focusing the mind on the requirements to be addressed in formulating a contingency plan.

> *Note* *This is not intended to be a comprehensive plan, merely an example to illustrate areas of concern and a means of approach.*

The problem

A company produces high-value widgets which need careful handling and storage and have a relatively short shelf life. They are sold throughout the UK and there is a growing export market to immediately adjacent European countries (which are supplied direct). The company occupies three factories (two freehold and one leasehold; one large, two small) as well as a main warehouse (leasehold) plus a number of satellite warehouses supplying retail customers within 24 hours of order.

The production process is partly mechanised but does require a certain amount of manual work. Since the manual operation requires a certain dexterity, this part of the workforce is mainly female and essentially part-time. Flexibility of hours has been a recruiting guideline for some years. The recession has led to a lengthening list of debtors despite constant chasing by the credit control department. Meanwhile, there has been a constant rise in raw material costs and difficulty (again because of the recession) in passing these on in the form of price increases to the market. Formerly a small amount of raw material was derived as a by-product of animal experimentation, but this has not been the case for several years.

Certain anonymous terrorist threats have been made against the company and a number of small incendiary devices have been received via the post at head office, one of the factories and the warehouse.

The Board is concerned that its operations could become a target for some serious (i.e. large-scale) terrorist activity and has asked you to prepare a report highlighting areas of weakness and vulnerability, suggesting initiatives that could be taken to defuse the situation and, should such activity occur, to recover the status quo.

Suggested areas of attention

> <u>Note</u> It should be noted that these are not exhaustive but are provided as examples of areas to be considered.

1. Worst-case scenario

Assess what is likely to be the worst disaster to hit the company and consider action, then next worst and so on. In this case it could be said that the worst case would occur should all productive units be wiped out simultaneously. This is probably so unlikely that it can be safely ignored. However the next worst case could envisage the main factory being wiped out, followed possibly by the head office going and so on.

Therefore, the problem to be addressed is to assume that the main factory no longer exists (see 6 below).

2. Research enemy

Trying to establish who or what is likely to be the enemy (whether animate in terms of this example, or inanimate in terms of a fire, etc.), what they need and what their aims are will help establish ways of dealing with the perceived problem. For example, if the Animal Liberation Front were suspected, it might be possible to contact them to confirm the cessation of the work which seems to be the source of their complaints. In the case of fire, it must be realised that fire needs three factors before it can cause damage – a source, raw material and time. If any of these are absent – the electrical wiring is checked regularly, materials are stored safely and sprinklers are installed – there can be little threat from such a source.

3. Consider advantages

The way this particular group is geographically spread provides an advantage. It has a number of sites and it is extremely unlikely that all

CONTINGENCY PLANNING

could be hit simultaneously. Assuming the organisation wishes to retain such a multiplicity of sites, the development of flexibility of roles could be addressed, so that if one site is disabled another can cover, at least temporarily. Conversely, any inter-dependability of sites could be reduced.

4. Take advice

No one can be expert in all areas. There are experts specialising in this field and their input could be sought. Even though the plan developed may never be used, the examination of procedures and practices may almost amount to a miniprocess re-engineering survey generating benefits of immediate use and value.

5. Examine vulnerability

(a) Post – institute controls and examination; arrange for parcels and packages to be delivered elsewhere and passed to premises only when opened safely.

(b) Access – examine security generally (entrances and exits, control, etc.).

(c) Deliveries – institute letters of authority to ensure access provided only to genuine suppliers.

(d) Publicity – promote 'clean hands' aspect of process.

(e) Screen employees – check references, institute right of search, control internal access to sensitive areas, maintain records of unsatisfactory employees.

(f) Increase internal security precautions – fire, explosion, etc. (creation of 'safe' areas).

(g) Ensure that the rear entrances of units are not identified.

6. Consider means of recovery

(a) Relocation of workforce – consider 'bussing' people in difficult in view of nature of employment.

(b) Possibility of production at warehouses.

(c) Need to check/circumvent lease restrictions.

(d) Keep watch on local property market to establish what is available.

(e) Buy in product/assembly.

(f) Homeworking (check security and quality control).

(g) Media messages and spokesperson.

(h) Parallel working particularly of computer system (credit control is especially vulnerable).

Covenants

> **Introduction**
>
> Much of the content of the average lease comprises paragraphs setting out covenants given by one party to the other. Covenants are binding undertakings and experience indicates that many lessees tend either to ignore them in considering the terms of a lease or to give them only cursory attention then – and even less attention during the lease. However, failure to observe the covenants can result in a breach of the lease. This in turn could lead to the loss of rights – e.g. the right to exercise an OPTION TO BREAK the term.

Lessee's covenants

Payment

a) Rent. Understandably the most common, and perhaps the most obvious, covenant requires the lessee to pay rent on the due dates. The dates will be set out in the lease and will normally be the four quarter days although there may be regional variations. Some leases may allow days of grace regarding payment (e.g. rent must be paid within 14 days of the due date) although this practice is dying out and increasingly not only is rent required to be paid on the due date but any late payment will attract interest often at penal rates (e.g. several percentage points over base rate). Rent is usually due whether demanded or not and thus the non-receipt of a demand for rent is not a valid reason for late or non-payment. Investigation should be made of the manner of charging for odd days at the beginning or end of a lease since there can be a variation in the charges levied depending whether the calculation is made on a per day basis (the rent divided by 365) or proportion of a quarter (the rent divided by 4 and then divided by the number of days in a quarter).

b) VAT registration. Since 1989, rent can be made subject to VAT at the option of the landlord. If the lessee is VAT registered, apart from cash flow, this may have little effect on the business, but it could have a severe effect on non-VAT registered lessees (e.g. charities). For such

51

prospective lessees whether VAT is demanded on the rent may be a material factor in deciding whether to take the lease.

c) Other outgoings. Normally the lessee will be responsible for paying for heating and lighting as well as the rates applicable to the property (or at least their part of it) as well as any insurance and service charges levied by the landlord. Most landlords prefer to insure the property in their own name and to pass on to the lessee the premium cost. The decision in the case of *Havenbridge Ltd v Boston Dyers Ltd* was that there is no obligation on the landlord to 'shop around' to gain the cheapest premium although it may be prudent for a lessee, if a premium is thought to be excessive to obtain an equivalent quote and approach the landlord and/or the insurers to try to gain a reduction.

d) SERVICE CHARGES. Where the property is occupied by a number of lessees, each lessee will be responsible for part of the costs of maintaining, heating, lighting and cleaning those parts of the premises which are used by all lessees. A check should be made to ensure that should one (or more) lessee not pay, the shortfall cannot be recouped from other lessees.

e) Landlord's costs. Often leases specify that the lessee will pay any charges incurred by the landlord. Whilst this may be fair where the matter arises as a result of the volition of the lessee – e.g. permission is required for alterations to the property and a deed is prepared, or where the lessee is in default, e.g. non-compliance with repairing covenants leading to the preparation of a SCHEDULE OF DILAPIDATIONS, it may be considered invidious for the landlord to expect the lessee to pay for legal and other costs incurred by the landlord in effecting a rent review or lease renewal. This should be negotiated when the lease is granted. The Cost of Leases Act 1959 laid down the dictum that each side should be responsible for its own legal costs.

Notes

(i) *When negotiating the lease terms it may be possible to agree that the lessee can be responsible for insurance although the landlord will normally wish to see evidence of renewal of the cover and to have their interest entered on the policy.*

(ii) *If the landlord insures then the lessee should ask for their interest to be endorsed on the policy. This is particularly important if the lease is 'full repairing' as, if there is partial or complete damage to the property, any shortfall in the landlord's insurance may be attempted to be recovered from the lessees.*

(iii) *The amount to be reclaimed in respect of any service charge should be checked for content by referring to the items stated in the lease as being the responsibility of the lessee. The actual amounts included should also be checked as should any proportion applied (if the charge covers other users).*

Condition

a) Redecoration and repair. Most leases include redecoration and repairing clauses as well as an obligation on the lessee to hand back the premises in a reasonable state. If the lease contains full repairing obligations, then, even if the premises were in a poor state when the lease started (or the lessee acquired the right of occupation on ASSIGNMENT or UNDERLETTING), the property must be handed back in a good state. This is particularly the case if the repairing covenant includes the word 'put' as well as 'keep' in good repair. Effectively this means the lessee could finish up paying for betterment – putting the property in a better condition than it was when they first became responsible. Whilst repair is an ongoing obligation, redecoration tends to be linked to set periods, – e.g., redecorate externally every three years and internally every five years (or equivalent). In practice few landlords seem to check to ensure redecorating covenants have been complied with. However increasingly checks are made regarding compliance with repairing covenants. To ensure that the lessee complies with these a landlord may prepare a schedule of works and require the lessee to carry out such works to return the premises to a well-repaired/decorated state. This schedule of 'wants of repair' is usually termed a Schedule of Dilapidations.

Notes

(i) *On negotiating a lease it may be possible to minimise the effect of such covenants by agreeing a SCHEDULE OF CONDITION. This is a statement showing the state of repair of the premises when the lease started/occupation commenced and acts as a criteria of the level of redecoration/repair which (but not beyond) the lessee must meet.*

(ii) *Until recently a lessee in receipt of a Schedule of Dilapidations in the early part of a lease could attempt to mitigate its effect (in full or in part) by arguing that, since the lease had a considerable time to run, the interests of the landlord were not being prejudiced for failure to comply with the repairing covenants (although it should not be overlooked that a landlord might wish to dispose of the interest in the lease and therefore their interests could be prejudiced by the lessee's failure to comply with such covenants).*

However, in the case of Jervis v Harris it was held that despite there being

> *a considerable time left before expiry (in this case around 900 years) and it being likely that at the time of expiry the building might not be in existence, the onus was still on the tenant (lessee) to comply with the repairing covenants. Further, in the event of failure, the landlord had the right to enter the premises to carry out the works and to recover the costs as a debt.*

> (iii) *The extent of any repairing and redecorating covenant must be clearly delineated. This can range from total responsibility for the whole building – both internal and external – to internal responsibility for the small area actually occupied or even to nil responsibility. In multi-occupation buildings it is normal for each lessee to bear some responsibility for a proportion of the cost of repair of the roof (rather than this being left as the responsibility of the lessee of the top floor). This can be achieved either by a specific covenant or by requiring a contribution to a service charge.)*

(b) Alterations or extensions. Normally there will be a bar on the lessee carrying out any alterations or extensions (LESSEE'S WORKS), etc., to the premises by the lease, or at least a bar subject to the landlord's permission being obtained prior to the commencement of any such works.

(c) REINSTATEMENT. Should the lessee carry out such works then normally as a condition of the grant of the landlord's approval of the works, the lessee will be required to put the property back to its state before the works (that is the works must be removed and the site made good).

(d) Keep safe. The lessee is using the landlord's property and there is an implied requirement, often included as a covenant, that the premises will be kept safe and, when not in use, will be secured and protected.

Keep open and use

(a) Hours of trade. Whilst particularly a requirement for the retail trade, a number of non-retail use leases include an obligation to keep the premises open for certain hours per day and to close them thereafter. Provided the hours stipulated are in accord with those preferred by the lessee this should pose no problem. However, any restrictions should be closely examined in case it is necessary to negotiate an 'opt-out'.

COVENANTS

> **WARNING** Until 1996 this covenant was not thought too onerous. Two recent court cases have forced a rethink of this requirement.
>
> (i) in the *Co-op v Argyll Stores* case, the Court of Appeal held that Argyll (trading as Safeway) was obliged to keep open its unit in the Hillsborough Shopping Centre at Sheffield, even though the company, presumably since it was unprofitable, had closed it.
>
> (ii) In the *Retail Parks Investments Ltd v Royal Bank of Scotland plc*, the bank was held to be in breach of the covenant in closing a branch and merely leaving two automatic cash dispensing machines operative at a location. The Court of Session held that it could make an order forcing the Bank to keep its branch open.

(b) Use for type of trade. Many leases include an obligation to use the premises only for the purpose stated in the lease (that is the purpose set out in any 'USER CLAUSE'). If it is likely that the purpose for which the lessee wishes to use the property could change (or the lessee may wish to assign to a third party who may want to use the premises for another purpose), then endeavours should be made to have written into this clause wording such as 'to use for [designated purpose] and such other use as may be permitted by the landlord, such permission not to be unreasonably withheld'. With this proviso included, then as long as the new use is reasonable, the landlord should not be able to object.

Notes

   (i)   The question of whether to have a restricted or wide user clause may be double-edged. With a restricted clause it may be possible to argue that the rent on review should be restricted – because comparison should only be made with other similar users. Conversely, if flexibility is retained with the 'such other use' wording the rent review valuation can rely on other users which may inflate the figure.

   (ii) If there is a restricted user clause, then the provisions of the rent review clause need to be examined to ensure that the effect of the restriction is to be taken account of during the review negotiations.

   (iii) Whilst the appeal of the restricted user clause may be considerable, it should not be overlooked that any change to the use will need the permission of the landlord. Applying for such a change of use may provide an opportunity for the landlord to attempt to vary the rent. The landlords of some of the outlets stocking the then new National Lottery in late 1994 and in 1995 attempted to argue that this was an extension

> *of the user of the premises and their permission was needed for this use. A few even succeeded in obtaining additional rent as a 'quid pro quo'.*

(c) Reasonable use. A number of covenants may be included covering:

(i) bans on the storage of dangerous material (a definition of 'dangerous' should be sought and compared with the requirements of the lessee's business).

(ii) requirements not to overload the floor(s). In this case written clarification of the floor loading should be sought since lack of the provision of such a statistic (as in many cases it is unknown) may tend to negate the impact of the covenant).

(iii) a ban on using the premises for immoral purposes, to hold auctions and other (depending on circumstances) specific purposes.

(iv) bans on fixing advertisement hoardings to the exterior of the premises. This is usually diluted so that the normal trade displays are allowed provided they are kept within certain dimensions, etc.

Maintain occupation

(a) Not to leave vacant. Vacant buildings tend to deteriorate quickly, apart from often becoming targets for vandalism. Lessees are thus usually required to occupy and keep the premises occupied other than for short periods. Permission from the landlord is normally needed if the lessee needs to leave the property vacant for any appreciable length of time. If, without permission, the premises are left vacant at or just before the termination of the lease then the lessee may lose any rights to a new lease.

> <u>Note</u> *In the case of Graysim Holdings v P&O Property Holdings Ltd the House of Lords held that a landlord was entitled not to grant a new lease to a lessee who were no longer in occupation having sublet the entire premises.*

(b) Bar on assignment. A lease is a contract between the parties and occupation under it is a right given only to the lessee. Such a right cannot be transferred without the consent of the landlord. Some leases will simply state that the leasehold interest cannot be transferred and although there is nothing to stop the lessee asking for such permission the landlord may be able to resist any moves to assign or part with possession. If the lessee wishes to retain flexibility the wording of this covenant needs to be diluted 'not to assign or part with possession of part, or, without the permission of the landlord such permission not to be unreasonably withheld, not to assign or part with possession of the whole'.

(c) Bar on underletting. A similar prohibition on underletting may be included. Underletting may be a more attractive proposition to assignment since should the underlessee default, at least the lessee still has control of the property and can either try to find another underlessee or re-occupy themselves. Whilst it may be possible to obtain a relaxation of any bar against subletting the whole, few landlords may allow subletting of part of the property, basically since this tends to detract from the investment value of the property as well as leading to potential problems in its management.

> *Note* In the event that underletting is permitted, a further covenant requiring all the covenants in the lease to be repeated in any underlease may also be included.

(d) Peaceful occupation. Many leases, particularly where the premises are in multi-occupation require the lessees to occupy their premises peaceably (i.e. with due regard for the neighbours). Not only is this courteous, it also makes the management of the premises much easier.

(e) Surrender occupation on the due date (i.e. by the expiry of the lease).

Communicate

Being in occupation the lessee will have control of receipt of post and other items delivered to the premises. Since some communications sent to the address will be for the owner rather than the occupier there is normally a requirement for the lessee to pass such items to the landlord within a reasonable time (or even 'immediately').

Indemnity

This entails the lessee confirming they will indemnify the landlord in respect of all occurrences arising out of their occupation of the premises.

Landlord's covenants

Maintain

Where a property is in multi-occupation, the landlord will normally retain some residual responsibility for maintenance of the common parts the cost of which may or may not be passed on to the lessees. In the case of *British Telecom v Sun Life Assurance*, it was held that a landlord had to comply with such a covenant 'at all times' and could not delay compliance for a 'reasonable time'.

Insure

Unless the lessee has negotiated permission to arrange their own insurance, the landlord will normally retain the right and responsibility for arranging insurance whilst passing the actual cost on to the lessee.

General notes

1. The foregoing provides an outline of and guide to the covenants found most generally in leases. This does not mean the list is exhaustive. In addition to a selection of or all of the above individual leases may contain additional covenants. It is important that all covenants and their effect on the actual operation of the subject business (not just their legal effect) are considered and understood.

2. A brief summary of the most important covenants should be included in any lease PRECIS and known and understood by all involved in the occupation and administration of the premises.

Dilapidations, Schedule of

Introduction

Most leases contain repairing COVENANTS which require the lessee to keep the premises demised by the lease in a state of reasonable repair. Some leases go further than this and place on the lessee an obligation to 'put and keep in repair' which means that, regardless of the state of the property (and irrespective of the culpability of another person in letting the property deteriorate to that state), they are liable for the works required to bring the property to a reasonable state of repair immediately they become responsible for it. Since many lessees overlook (deliberately or in ignorance) such covenants, landlords reserve to themselves the right at any time during the term to serve on the lessee a schedule of wants of repair or, as it is more commonly termed a Schedule of Dilapidations.

Timing

Schedules of Dilapidations can be served at any time during the term of the lease and will usually stipulate a time within which the works must be completed. Having accepted that such a schedule can be served at any time, if challenged the landlord could previously be required to prove that damage is being caused to their interests by the lessee's failure to repair the property. For example, in the first few years of a 25 year lease a landlord might have been unable to prove that his interests were being damaged by the lessee's failure to repair a dilapidated area within the property. However, near the end of the lease, or when the landlord was trying to sell his interest, proving that the interest was damaged might be more feasible. However, in the case of *Jervis v Harris*, the Court of Appeal found that although it was unlikely that the building would be standing at the end of the lease (which had around 900 years to run) the lessee was still required to comply with the repairing obligations and that, in the event of failure, the landlord had a right of entry to the premises, to carry out the work and to recover the costs from the lessee as a debt.

During the slump in demand for property in the early 1990s which was allied to the recession, many institutional landlords became so concerned that lessees might go out of business having failed to maintain the property that the serving of schedules increased considerably.

Content

Normally a surveyor will be appointed by the landlord to inspect the property and compile a schedule of those matters requiring attention. Such a schedule must be compiled by reference to the terms of the lease and in accordance with the extent of the repairing and redecorating covenants set out therein. Thus, in a single-occupation, full-repairing lease, every aspect of the property from the roof to the basement that is considered to be in unreasonable condition could be listed. Because an item is listed, however, does not necessarily mean that it must be dealt with, or dealt with to the extent required. There is normally some leeway and the possibility of negotiation regarding the extent.

It may be possible to challenge the detail of the work required in accordance with some old leases. For example, wordings such as 'paint with three coats of good-quality oil-based paint' have been rendered redundant by modern paints and most landlords will agree that an undercoat plus a coat of a good quality gloss paint is all that is now needed.

Negotiation

Once a schedule has been served, the lessee needs to assess its content. With a short schedule of relatively minor works it may be counterproductive to argue the content as the time wasted in arguing could outweigh the costs of the works. Even with a longer schedule careful thought needs to be given to the idea of employing a surveyor to negotiate. Although most surveyors may be able to reduce the extent and effect of the list, they will charge for this service and unless a list seems unduly padded or is very extensive or relates to a large property, it may be that the value of the reductions will not exceed the costs of the surveyor.

Deal

The serving of a schedule, particularly near the end of a lease, does not necessarily mean that a lessee needs to obtain quotes, etc., for the work, since some landlords instead of requiring completion will place a value on the works and offer the lessee the choice of having the works done themselves or paying the agreed value of the works. If the lessee's occupation is to finish in any event, then providing that a suitably worded agreement is prepared it may be more convenient for the lessee to pay the sum agreed since this will save all the dislocation during the last period of occupation and the costs of supervising the works. The advantage to the landlord is that he has a cash sum and it is not unknown for the premises to be re-let without any of the works covered by the Schedule of Dilapidations being completed. The obligations to repair, etc., are simply passed on to the new lessee and the landlord retains the money.

> *Note*   *In such a situation the new lessee should argue that to offset the costs of putting the premises into a decent condition a rent-free period or some other 'sweetener' should be allowed.*

There may be a temptation when attempting to avoid the work involved in carrying out the repairs and whilst ensuring an appropriately worded agreement is drafted, not to look too closely at the schedule itself. Every schedule should be scrutinised to ensure it complies with the lease requirements and contains only reasonable items. Further, (an) alternative quote(s) should be obtained for carrying out the work to ensure the figure offered as an alternative is itself fair.

Schedule of condition

Where a prospective lessee is in a strong bargaining position it may be possible to argue that a Schedule of Condition should be prepared. In this instance any Schedule of Dilapidations can only require the lessee to bring the property to the standard evidenced by the Schedule of Condition. Most landlords dislike the idea of properties protected by Schedules of Condition because, as they limit the effect of the full repairing covenants, the potential value of the landlord's investment is impaired.

Service

The manner of serving the schedule, as well as the liability for the costs of its preparation, will be laid down in the lease. Often the costs of the preparation are required to be passed to the lessee. In addition, it may be stipulated that the lessee is required to acknowledge receipt of such a schedule. The date of such receipt may also start the period within which the works must be completed (although often leases are silent on the time to be allowed for completion).

Default

If the lessee is in default in failing to comply with the requirements of a Schedule of Dilapidations, the landlord may have recourse to the law. If the lease has expired then the landlord would be entitled not only to recover from the lessee the value of the works in order to bring the property to an acceptable state (i.e. an amount which reflects the damage to the landlord's interest) but also a sum related to the rent for the property which will be lost for the duration of the works.

Disposal

> **Introduction**
>
> Whilst considerable attention is rightly given to the acquisition of property, often too little attention is given to its disposal, particularly where there has been a RELOCATION and the property is surplus to requirements. 'Out of sight, out of mind' is a saying which springs to mind in such circumstances. Considering both the value that can be invested in a property as well as the potential costs of damage from vandalism, etc., this should not become the property administrator's attitude.

Administration

In acquiring a property the organisation has control of the situation. Having found a site it can within limits speed up or slow down the timetable to completion and occupation and, should it eventually change its mind concerning the subject property, it can actually walk away from the whole deal. Conversely, with disposal, the organisation is locked into the property until some other organisation or person completes on the sale and purchase. The timetable is not usually under the vendor's control particularly as most areas of the UK in the recent past have experienced a glut of available property leading to the creation of a buyer's market. Realisation of the situation should encourage the administrator to remove as much of the delay which tends to be endemic in property transactions. Often delay is caused simply because necessary information is not available. Therefore, the greater the preparation, the more likely the ability to shorten the stages between interest and completion. The stages are listed below.

(a) Compile file containing all relevant information. This would include: plans of building (or appropriate part), layouts, occupation details, decisions re sale of equipment, alarms etc., details of wayleaves (e.g. permission to pass over part of the property given to a third party), consents, planning permissions, etc. Obviously generating this information should be rendered more simple if there is available a good-quality PROPERTY REGISTER or records.

(b) Prepare list of extras, equipment, fixtures and fittings, etc., to be left with the building specifying whether these are included in the sale price. It may be better to ignore such items initially and, should the demand be slight or the disposal become bogged down in detail, offer to include such extras in the sale price, provided swift agreement exchange completion can be obtained.

> *Note* It may be cost-effective to transfer contracts, particularly of vending machines, etc., with lengthy termination clauses, to the new occupiers although some negotiation may be necessary.

(c) Instruct agents to dispose having first checked the basis for payment, and whether fee includes or excludes charges for expenses and/or advertising. If advertising is charged as an extra, agree budget and campaign. Specify time limit for sole agency and review effectiveness near end of such limit. Insist on regular written updates of progress (even if there is a lack of progress).

(d) Instruct solicitors of decision to dispose, deliver title or occupation deeds so they can commence preparation of contract, requests for consent to assign (leased property), etc. It may also be helpful for the solicitors to list all the contract enquiries they expect to be asked by a purchaser and to originate the replies. Anticipating requests in this way provides more time later in the process when time is tight since researching the answers can be very time-consuming.

(e) Prepare analysis of water rates and utility charges, and provide these to agents with copies of latest payments. Most prospective purchasers will want some guidance as to occupation costs no matter how unrelated these may be to their own business.

(f) List and prepare termination (or transfer) letters for telephone (may require intercept), telex and fax, computer link lines, alarm systems and vending machines. Some of these items may be better transferred to a purchaser to avoid any need to pay termination costs.

(g) Prepare details of any informal, or formal, agreements with neighbours. Formal arrangements will tend to be evidenced by legal agreements or contracts and should be easily sourced. However, informal arrangements which rest solely on recollection or verbal agreement can give rise to problems.

(h) Give notice to cease all janitorial services in accordance with contracts.

> *Note* As with a number of other items, it may be possible to transfer these to the purchasers but considering ceasing them at least brings their existence to mind.

(i) If the business has actually vacated the property being sold, it may be advisable to appoint someone to act as a caretaker and, whether agents have been appointed or not, to ensure that police and any other interested parties have a contact address for someone responsible for the property. It may be helpful to display this name at the premises – even casual passers-by have been known to buy properties.

(j) If disposing simultaneously of more than one property to the same purchaser either cover the sale of them all in one contract or keep each entirely separate and resist any suggestion that the sums involved should be linked. As well as making the disposal of each more simple, it should minimise the possibility of being caught by the device whereby a purchaser asks for a total sum previously agreed for a composite contract to be split as they wish between properties covered by separate sale contracts. They then proceed on the contract which provides them with an advantageous price on property A and, having exchanged contracts on that property, withdraw from contracts for properties B, C, etc.

Disposal of leases

Whilst most of the foregoing applies to a large extent whether the property is freehold or leasehold, the disposal of a lease (ASSIGNMENT) adds requirements to the checklist – not least the fact that the landlord will usually have the right to vet the proposed purchaser and thus the landlord must be asked to approve the purchaser before the assignment can take place. In view of the danger of being liable for outgoings related to the property should the assignee default under the PRIVITY OF CONTRACT rules, it may be better to consider UNDERLETTING to assignment.

Compulsory purchase

It should not be overlooked that an occupier and/or owner may sometimes find their own rights are subject to external authorities' rights, e.g. the wide powers nowadays devolved to planners. Planning authorities ultimately have the right of acquisition of premises needed to be cleared to allow a new road to be built. In such circumstances, the occupier/owner will be served with a Compulsory Purchase Order (CPO). Although there are rights of appeal against such a notice, the grounds of such appeal are limited. Expert advice should be sought in such a situation. The possibility of losing occupation in this way underlines the necessity of checking on planning developments both when considering purchase and then regularly during occupation.

Alternative methods of sale

Whilst marketing either direct or through agents is the most usual way of disposing of a property, such assets can also be sold by auction or by tender. With an auction the advantage is that a reserve price can be fixed with the property being withdrawn if that price is not exceeded. The costs are usually 10% of the price obtained which may exceed the costs charged by an agent. One major disadvantage when selling a property in which employees are still working is that whereas this can be done, within limits, reasonably confidentially via agents, an auction may be a high-profile event.

One way of avoiding the inevitable publicity of auctioning the property is by inviting interested parties to tender for the property. In effect the parties submit sealed bids to the owner who should stipulate that they do not have to accept the highest bid – or any of them. There are a number of pitfalls that can trap the unwary and advice from those experienced in the procedure should be sought.

Duties of Property Administrator

Introduction

Experience indicates that in many organisations, particularly the smaller ones, responsibility for property administration and control is thrust on to personnel, who, despite their capability and dedication, often have little or no experience of or training in property matters. The following list attempts to provide a reminder of the various duties and responsibilities that must be assumed in relation to the care and control of these assets – whether by the property administrator or by others. This list is cross-referenced to many of the sections within the book.

Checklist

(a) Administration of property records (including plans of all buildings updated to the most recent alterations) and their safe ARCHIVING.

(b) Devising (or assisting in the devising of) strategical planning of property requirements.

(c) Protecting rights, etc., e.g. rights under the LANDLORD AND TENANT ACT.

(d) Negotiating various rights and responsibilities, (e.g. under leases, licences and agreements).

(e) Relating to statutory bodies including PLANNING, BUILDING REGULATIONS, HEALTH & SAFETY, ENVIRONMENT authorities, etc.

(f) Obtaining and maintaining, if in a single occupation, a FIRE CERTIFICATE for the premises, or, in a multiple occupation ensuring the landlord has a current certificate.

(g) Meeting with landlord and/or agents.

(h) Meeting with bodies that have right of ACCESS, ensuring their rights are respected.

(i) Administration of building services, i.e. janitorial services including cleaning, security, reception, safety, etc.

(j) Formulating specifications and job descriptions for employees responsible for cleaning, security, reception, etc., and/or specifications for bought-in services.

(k) Ensuring compliance with fire regulations, checking fire escape routes are clear, testing fire bells or alarms, setting up procedure for fire drills and ensuring problems are eradicated.

(l) Ensuring compliance with redecoration and repairing COVENANTS in leasehold premises and/or formulating and complying with such a schedule if freehold.

(m) Ensuring janitorial provisions as part of risk assessment/prevention procedure.

(n) Meeting with insurers and carrying out their requirements, e.g. regarding lifts, boilers, etc. which have statutory implications; making claims.

(o) Commissioning/overseeing BUILDING WORKS and/or subcontractors.

(p) Meeting with utilities, arranging contracts with gas and electricity suppliers, and control of heating, ventilation, communication, etc., systems.

> *Note* This could include precautions required regarding Legionnaire's and other diseases which could entail regular cleansing of water and holding tanks, etc.

(q) Responsibility for security and for preparing sabotage and bomb threat procedures and ensuring those affected know the action required.

(r) Responsibility for preparing or being involved in the preparation of CONTINGENCY or disaster plans.

(s) Ensuring compliance with safety requirements.

(t) Meeting with NEIGHBOURS and dealing with TRESPASSERS.

(u) Considering and taking action re notices and schedules received from LANDLORDS, e.g. RENT REVIEWS, SCHEDULES OF DILAPIDATIONS, etc.

(v) Overseeing the ACQUISITION of new facilities.

(w) Overseeing the DISPOSAL (or ASSIGNMENT/UNDERLETTING) of redundant facilities.

(x) Overseeing commissioning of and relocation to new facilities.

(y) Interpreting the effect of legal decisions and actioning changes where necessary.

(z) Analysing the effect of and implementing the requirements of legislation.

Environment Protection

Introduction

Recent pressure of both public opinion and of legislation originating from the European Union has led to an enhanced interest in and desire to protect the environment from 'damage' occasioned to it by business. The Environmental Protection Act 1990 represented a development of the various statutory requirements that were already in place, a restructuring of requirements regarding pollution control and waste management and the commencement of increasingly stringent regulations concerning the protection of the environment. The effects of that Act were enhanced by the Environment Act 1995. The following is a resume of the main effects of both Acts.

Integrated Pollution Control (IPC)

This requires those creating pollution to consider alternative means of containing the release of pollutants by using the 'best available techniques not entailing excessive cost' (the BATNEEC concept). IPC was phased in over five years commencing 1 April 1991 and involves the regulation of all forms of emissions of pollutants and their cross-assessment so that the Best Practicable Environmental Option is determined, i.e. that levels of emissions to be released are determined and the most appropriate media of absorption is decided. Under current legislation, the Health and Safety (Emissions into the Atmosphere) Regulations 1983, a person in control of premises in which a process emitting pollutants into the atmosphere is conducted has a duty to use the best practical means to prevent such emission and to render the emissions harmless. Emission levels are being published and will be made mandatory with criminal sanctions for breach. In addition, all relevant information will be made public and members of the public will be able to bring prosecutions individually. Compulsory insurance cover (likely to be expensive) will also be required.

Waste management

Those undertaking waste disposal have a 'duty of care' to:

(a) prevent unlawful deposits or act other than in accordance with and as authorised by a licence.

(b) prevent the escape of waste.

(c) transfer waste to an authorised person, with an accurate and adequate written description to enable the transferee to deal with the waste.

A code of practice has been issued to help courts determine whether these duties have been discharged. Breach of the duty is a criminal offence with a maximum fine of £20,000. Licences for waste disposal will only be issued to 'fit and proper' persons, who should be technically qualified, have appropriate financial resources and should not have been previously convicted of a relevant criminal offence. Those generating waste have an obligation to ensure that their waste is processed by a 'fit and proper' person. Since only fit and proper persons will have licences, there is an onus on all property occupiers to check that their waste remover has a current licence, and one which covers the type of waste they are generating.

> *Note* This obligation is placed on all creators of waste other than domestic residents.

The Secretary of State for the Environment publishes strategies aiming at reducing the production of waste and the risk of pollution or harm to human health from waste disposal or recovery. The aim is both to generate less waste and to recycle more.

> **WARNING** Companies with over 200 employees will soon be required to publish environmental policies covering waste and produce systems to give effect to them.

The Secretary of State is also empowered to make regulations concerning 'producer responsibility' in order to increase the re-use, recovery and/or recycling of products or material for which initiative there is increasing pressure from the European Community.

Waste carriers

Registration with the local authority in which area the principal place of business is situated is required of anyone who transports waste. Registers giving details of all carriers are maintained by the authority and are open to free inspection by the public.

ENVIRONMENT PROTECTION

Contaminated land

Although the original proposal contained in the 1990 Act was scrapped mainly since those involved in the property market (and others) feared the effect would be a serious land blight, a diluted version of the concept was introduced in the 1995 Act.

The main points are listed below.

(a) Where there is contaminated land, remedial action will be required where there is 'significant harm' or 'pollution of controlled waters' and there are cost-effective methods of cleansing.

(b) Local authorities must identify land within their boundaries which is contaminated. Heavily contaminated land will be classified as 'special sites' requiring special provisions. Following a three-month 'consultation period', the local authority can serve a remediation notice on the 'appropriate person'. If this notice is not complied with then the authority can enter the land and cleanse it recovering the costs from the 'appropriate person'. It can place a charge in its favour on the land if these costs are not reimbursed.

(c) The 'appropriate person' is the person who caused the contamination. Of course this may not be the owner although if the polluter cannot be found it may be the owner who has to pay.

Air pollution

The Secretary of State can set standards, reduction targets and timetables on a national basis. Local authorities will have similar powers related to the areas under their control.

Water pollution

When water has been (or could be) polluted, the Environment Agency (formed in April 1996 as a result of the 1995 Act) can serve a notice requiring anti-pollution action. No longer will the defendant have the right to a sample of the water being used as evidence of the pollution (which could be independently analysed).

> **WARNING** Companies having emissions into water might be well advised to sample the target water regularly and to keep the dated samples.

> *Note* Current draft EU proposals would require companies in 58 industries to produce annual audits of their environmental performance at every site.

Fire Procedure

Introduction

Unless they have been involved in a fire, most people seem affected by a law of inertia on hearing a fire alarm. To ensure prompt evacuation such inertia must be overcome. This can be achieved by means of constant practice, so that on hearing the alarm the automatic response is to move rather than hesitate. Such movement may need to be hastened by specially appointed employees acting as fire marshals (and deputies to cover absences). Regular fire alarm tests and even fire drills (expected to be made mandatory under proposed legislation) should be conducted.

Policy

The organisation's fire policy (or instructions to be followed in the event of fire) should be formulated and disseminated to all employees and all recruits as soon as possible after starting.

1. Procedure and advice

The alarm is tested every week/month at [time] a.m./p.m. Familiarise yourself with the alarm and, should it ring other than at these times, follow the evacuation procedure IMMEDIATELY.

Details of the primary and back-up evacuation routes of each department are posted within the department. You MUST familiarise yourself with such routes.

Each department has a fire marshal and deputy to oversee all evacuations. All employees must comply with instructions issued by fire marshals or deputies.

2. Drills

Fire drills are held [monthly]. When the alarm sounds for a drill or at an unexpected time (i.e. other than on a test):

(a) switch off your machine if it is safe to do so and close any windows in the immediate vicinity.

(b) proceed to the department's primary evacuation route, or, if the primary route is blocked, to the secondary route.

(c) after evacuation, assemble in the designated assembly point for your department and ensure your name is checked by the Fire Marshal (or deputy) – follow the Marshal's (or deputy's) instructions.

(d) do NOT return to the building or attempt to move a car from the car park unless instructed to do so.

(e) DON'T RUN, DON'T PANIC, DON'T USE LIFTS, DON'T VISIT CLOAKROOMS or collect bags, etc.

3. Discovery

If you discover a fire:

(a) operate the nearest Fire Alarm call point.

(b) if there is no immediate danger to life, attack the fire with the appliances supplied.

(c) if the fire seems to be gaining a hold, or life is threatened in any way, abandon such fire-fighting activities and evacuate.

(d) make any knowledge, of the fire, its origins, seat, etc., known to fire fighters.

WARNING Implementation of the Fire Precautions (Places of Work) Regulations 1992 which contain far-reaching requirements is awaited. When implemented, employers should ensure they are aware of and comply with them, since injury or death as a result of non-compliance could lead to substantial claims.

Fire Certificate

Introduction

A certificate is required to be issued by the Fire Officer for all buildings used for work as are covered by the Fire Precautions (Factories, Offices, Shops and Railway Premises) Order 1988. Buildings where the public are admitted for entertainment are covered under other regulations. Currently certificates are issued provided the occupier/owner has complied with the requirements issued by the Fire Officer. However under the Fire Precautions (Places of Work) Regulations 1992 due to be implemented in the near future, employers will need to be proactive rather than reactive in this area. This means that occupiers will be responsible for assessing requirements and protections in accordance with the regulations rather than waiting for the Fire Officer to issue or update requests and then reacting to such requests.

Responsibility

The responsibility for obtaining a certificate depends upon the occupancy of each building. If the business is in sole occupation it is the responsibility of the occupier to obtain the certificate. Conversely, if is there is shared occupation, the responsibility is that of the owner.

Adequate and accurate information must be supplied by the person responsible to the Fire Officer. It is an offence to give information recklessly or knowing it to be false. Any requirements stipulated by the Fire Officer must be complied with. Any alterations of use of the premises, or any alterations to the structure, or any possibility that flammable or explosive materials will be stored in the premises, must be notified to the Fire Officer. The person responsible must provide adequate means of escape and fire-fighting equipment (whether or not a certificate has been granted).

A certificate must be obtained by the person responsible if more than 20 people are employed, or if more than ten are employed on a floor other than the ground floor, or if flammable or explosive materials are stored (regardless of numbers employed). If a certificate has not been applied for (or has been refused) the premises may not be used for that purpose. Once the certificate has been obtained, the premises may only be used in accordance with its requirements and restrictions.

Access

The Fire Officer must be allowed total access to all parts of the building before and after the grant of a certificate.

Display

A copy of the current certificate must be kept at the subject premises.

Means of escape

The certificate will specify means of escape and fire-fighting appliances required. Appliances must be supplied with adequate notices and appropriate markings of fire escape routes, etc. Fire fighting appliances and equipment must be regularly maintained. It is advisable to conduct regular fire evacuation practices as much to test the escape routes as the response of the employees. Requirements regarding regular fire alarm tests and drills may be recommended/required by the Fire Officer.

Pre-certificate issue

A Fire Officer will usually indicate his outline requirements to allow occupation pending grant of a certificate. These requirements must be complied with.

First Aid

Introduction

Whilst perhaps mainly the preserve of the personnel or occupational health functions in an organisation, the provision of first aid is however very much linked to the property function not least since the extent/type of cover required is derived from the size and use of the building itself.

Philosophy

First aid can be defined as instant action carried out by (normally) minimally trained individuals in order to preserve life until attendance by a trained medical practitioner. Under no circumstances should those carrying out first aid initiate action which goes beyond the limits covered by this definition.

Suitably equipped first aid box(es) should be made available at each working location with suitably qualified persons being made responsible for it/them and for administering first aid.

Checklist for provision of first aid

Under the Health and Safety (First Aid) Regulations 1981 (and the code of practice issued in 1990), an employer must provide certain first aid facilities. These are as listed below.

1. Provide suitable first aid staff and services in accordance with the nature of the business, the degree of danger or hazard in the operations, the number of employees, and the proximity to medical assistance. As a guide, it is recommended that one first aider per 50 employees in a low-risk environment (e.g. office, shop, etc.) is adequate. If there are fewer than 50 employees, someone responsible should be appointed to act in the event of an incident. In higher-risk environments, it is required that there should be one first aider for up to 50 employees plus one first aider for every additional 50 employees. A first aider is defined as someone who holds a current certificate in first aid.

> *Note* *Consideration should be given to ensuring that there is at least one back-up first aider to ensure coverage during holidays and sickness.*

2. If there are 400 or more people employed at a single site, an employer will normally be required to provide a first aid room, but again its provision will depend on the assessment of the hazards.

3. Provide first aid boxes which will normally contain

    (a) a guidance card

    (b) 20 sterile adhesive dressing (assorted sizes)*

    (c) 2 sterile eye pads

    (d) 6 triangular bandages (for use as slings)

    (e) 6 safety pins*

    (f) 6 medium, 2 large and 3 extra large wound dressings.

    * In the food and catering industries, special detectable dressings, sharp objects (needles) etc. may be required.

All dressings, etc., should be individually wrapped and suitable protective gloves should be available. An airway may need to be provided for First Aiders concerned at possible HIV infection. Arrangements for the safe disposal of used and/or soiled dressings, sharp objects (e.g. needles) should be made and laid down as a procedure.

4. Details of the arrangements made regarding first aid must be made known to all employees. A suggested format is given below.

    (a) The organisation sponsors its first aiders by:

    (i) funding their training to acquire a certificate of competence, and any updating required.

    (ii) giving each first aider an annual honorarium of [£50] in recognition of their assistance.

    > *Note* *Point (a) has been included for example purposes only.*

    (b) There is a first aid room available for all employees who are required to rest for a pre-determined period. Such use must be authorised in advance by a manager or a first aider.

    (c) The duty of the first aiders is to preserve life until the attendance of a paramedic or qualified medical practitioner, to reassure the patient, and to ensure the speedy removal of the patient to hospital, in the event of a serious accident. First aiders are not permitted to issue drugs of any

FIRST AID

description, or to offer medical advice. No liability can be accepted by the organisation, or individual first aiders, for attending and helping in a situation requiring first aid.

(d) In the event of an accident or an employee feeling unwell – a supervisor should call a first aider who will treat the patient (as above) and enter, the patient's name, the nature of the accident or incident, the patient's condition and details of any treatment given, with a note of the time, date and place in the Accident Book.

(e) If the accident is a simple cut or abrasion, the first aider, or the patient, can clean the wound and apply an adhesive dressing. If the patient feels unwell, he or she should be taken to the first aid room, and allowed to sit or lie quietly for 30 minutes. If the feeling continues, the patient should be taken home, to his, or the organisation's, doctor or to hospital. Organisation transport should used rather than the employee's own vehicle. No liability will be accepted as a result of the organisation trying to assist in these ways. In the event that the employee's vehicle is left on organisation premises, efforts will be made to protect it, but no liability can be accepted for it.

(f) If a first aider considers an incident is serious, and that emergency treatment is required, he/or she will be responsible for summoning an ambulance. The first aider will brief the ambulance staff and, should the circumstances require, either the first aider, or a Personnel department representative, should accompany the employee to hospital, and either remain there until completion of treatment or until the family of the employee have been summoned, depending upon the circumstances.

(g) First aiders are expected to set an example by maintaining a high level of personal hygiene, e.g. washing their hands and changing dirty or soiled overalls, etc., before administering treatment of any kind. If a first aider needs to deal with bleeding, burns, sickness and is at risk of contact with bodily fluids, he or she should wear the protective gloves provided in every first aid box. Such gloves should be disposed of after treatment. Wearing protective clothes is good practice on all occasions when first aid is required . Any clothing which becomes soiled, should be removed as soon as appropriate and carefully cleaned. Any treatment dressings or swabs, etc., should be disposed of in appropriate containers.

(h) In the event of artificial resuscitation being required, an airway (provided in each first aid box) should be used rather than direct, mouth-to-mouth contact.

(i) Any first aider required to provide treatment, whilst bearing a cut or abrasion, should ensure such cuts, etc., are adequately protected.

(j) Each first aider will be responsible for a first aid box, and for the reordering of dressings so that the minimum contents are always available. Only a first aider should have access to a first aid box.

Fitting Out

Introduction

Although detailed attention is usually given to locating and acquiring occupation rights to a new building, experience indicates that often inadequate attention is given to customising and fitting out the premises so that they match the exact requirements of the business. It is impossible in this book to include more than a brief resume of some of the main (and most common) requirements to be addressed in this regard.

Permissions

The following permissions/consents/clearance may be required.

(a) Fire Officer.

(b) Public Health and/or Environmental Health. The requirements will depend on the use to which the building is put.

(c) Insurers. The requirements of insurers often run directly counter to those of the Fire Officer particularly regarding security provisions.

   Note It is usual and advisable to cover premises from the time of exchange of contracts, rather than from completion.

(d) Landlord's consent. Carrying out alterations to leased premises without the consent of the landlord (and any superior landlord) will usually be a breach of one or more of the lease COVENANTS. Landlord's permission will usually be obtained by means of a licence specifying the works, timetable, etc. In negotiating the terms of the permission, it is in the lessee's interests to try to ensure that any enhancement in value as a result of the works is excluded from future rent reviews. Any requirement to reinstate (i.e. to return the premises to their original state) should be resisted as far as possible or, at least, couched in terms which are practical. As an alternative, it may be possible to negotiate for the landlord to carry out the works and to rentalise the expenditure, i.e. to make an additional charge in respect of the works. This option (which has cash flow, increased rent, taxation and capital allowances' implications) needs careful examination.

(e) Planning consent and building regulations. These may be required even for the most modest alterations to the premises, and, since sanctions could include a requirement to remove the works, clearance should be sought.

(f) Petroleum officer. If petroleum spirit or diesel is to be stored on the premises, 'bunds' or retaining walls to contain spillages will be required.

Services

The services required for the efficient operation of the premises need to be identified and installed to the appropriate capacity allowing for at least some surplus to cover expansion and future flexibility. The range of such services will normally include the following.

(a) Electricity. The correct phase supply and amperage needs to be assessed, utilising power factor correction equipment if necessary. Computer systems normally require a clean level circuit and/or an uninterrupted power supply. Thus a battery or generator back-up power source or uninterrupted power supply equipment may be needed.

> Note   Generators tend to require a large space, can be noisy and create vibrations, and need to be run on test once a week. The power supply should be capable of coping with the demand at levels anticipated for at least three years.

(b) Gas. British Gas (and most alternative suppliers) require estimates of annual and shorter period consumptions and for a contract to be entered into. Since there are a number of alternative tariffs, estimating needs to be as accurate as possible. If a new main is to be laid it is essential to ensure it is of sufficient capacity to cope with demand for at least, say, ten years.

> Note   If there is no existing gas main, negotiations with neighbours may source additional potential users which could have the effect of spreading the initial cost.

(c) Compressed air. It will be more economical to make the original layout as comprehensive as possible to minimise disruption from later alteration/installation.

(d) Water. The water supply needs to be adequate for the demands of the business and it will usually be advisable to ensure the supply is metered. If a sprinkler system is to be installed it may be necessary to install a header tank to supplement the main pressure. Such a tank may require planning consent and will certainly require space.

(e) Heating, air conditioning and cooling equipment. The exact requirements need identifying and, since all tend to be costly, alternative methods should be costed.

Note *Although one energy source may appear more expensive than alternatives at lower levels of consumption, due to cost/consumption thresholds, it may be possible to achieve an overall price advantage by utilising a sole supplier for all uses.*

Takeover

If premises are being acquired with existing services, the project manager should ensure that meters are read as at completion date. The occupier will usually need to sign new customer forms for the utility suppliers.

Building works

1. Means of work

Alternative quotes for full contract, part contract (i.e. a number of suppliers taking responsibility for part of the contract under the control of the main contractor) or direct management works (where the occupier or a project manager employs a number of contractors to carry out the works on an individual project basis) should be obtained and properly documented. It may be advisable if time is short to tie contractors to penalties for late completion and/or to offer rewards for early completion. If a main contractor employs subcontractors, any contract should make it clear that responsibility for such subcontractors, and their payment, rests with the main contractor.

Although the direct management works may seem to be the cheapest alternative, the time/costs of scheduling different trades whilst progressing the work should not be underestimated. It may also be possible to negotiate on the initial estimates of the cost of the work, although care should be taken not to make the job so unattractive that the normal attention to progress is lacking.

2. Safety

Occupiers have a responsibility to ensure that contractors and subcontractors adopt and maintain safe working practices and do not breach health and safety legislation. The organisation's safety rules need to be supplied and explained to the contractors and their staff, who must be made to understand that they must work subject to such rules. The occupier cannot simply assume the contractors will work safely – there is an obligation to ensure this is the case.

> **WARNING** In addition, under the Construction (Design and Management) Regulations 1994 a health and safety plan must be prepared and a planning supervisor appointed to oversee it. The plan must be made available for inspection by interested parties. It should be noted that as well as a theoretical plan there should be physical precautions. In the case of *R. v Rhone-Poulenc Rorer Ltd*, the employer was found liable when a building contractor fell to his death through a rooflight. Although there were instructions, the court stated that the employer should have provided a guard-rail so that there was a physical obstruction as well as mere words.

3. Insurance cover

The agreement under which a contractor carries out the works will specify the amount of cover required and whether the name of the occupier needs to be endorsed on the policy. If a building is being erected from the foundations stage the contractor will be responsible for the building insurance cover until practical completion of the works. When alterations to an existing building are being effected the owner (freehold) or occupier or landlord (leasehold) will usually be responsible for the cover advising the insurers that contractors are working in the building. If the insurer loads the premium because of the works, the additional cost is usually passed to the contractor who will usually also insure the value of the works being carried out and be responsible for that premium. Confirmation of the contractor's insurance cover(s) should be obtained before the contract is signed.

Communication links

At the same time that the fitting out works are proceeding, it is necessary to order all required communication links so that their installation can be accommodated within the building work programme. Such services can include the following.

(a) External telephone service both through a switchboard and via direct lines for senior executives.

(b) Link line to separate premises if the amount of traffic is likely to be heavy. It will be necessary to survey demand.

(c) Fax, cable TV and/or telex links.

(d) Computer and/or modem link(s) to other premises, suppliers, agents and the Internet.

FITTING OUT

(e) Tied telephone lines for intruder/fire alarms.

(f) Internal telephone service.

(g) Internal computer links.

(h) TV aerial and satellite dish (may require consent).

(i) Appropriate word processing stations (with or without a computer link).

The planning of this part of the fitting out must be phased with the planning of the electrical supply layout, particularly regarding computer facilities – each VDU station requires at least a dual 13 amp socket in addition to the computer link itself. It is becoming increasingly common to run phone, computer and electrical supplies within a single duct – albeit with each item shielded from the other(s).

> *Note* Facilities management consultancy services are now available which can provide and supervise all these aspects of communication and data processing and recording.

Security protection

If fire and/or intruder alarm systems are not already installed they need to be commissioned and appropriate automatic telephone links arranged. Both the Fire Officer and the building insurers (as well as any landlord) may have an input on the exact requirements which often include the installation of smoke detectors. The Fire Officer will specify the number and type of fire extinguishers required as well as the number of fire exits, etc. It may also be advisable to install card access systems and/or closed circuit television systems to assist with the protection of the property.

Systems

A relocation or setting up in a new location provides an opportunity to re-examine existing systems and to make decisions regarding these including, for example, the storage and/or disposal of old files and records. It is important to avoid moving items which are no longer needed. Well in advance of a move every department in the organisation should be instructed to view objectively its existing equipment and storage, to prune such records as heavily as possible, and to assess future requirements. A senior executive should be appointed to oversee this project, acting in accordance with a predetermined retention/disposal policy. For items which must be kept, externally sourced repositories may be a more cost-effective alternative than storage within premises with a higher rent.

Administrative checklist

This is intended as a base only and will need to be individually customised.

(a) Ensure everyone involved knows the Project Manager and his or her mobile phone number.

(b) Arrange for telephone number to be allocated – retain existing or obtain a new 'memorable' number.

(c) Install an intercept on the previous number if not transferred.

(d) Obtain a postcode from Royal Mail.

(e) Print new notepaper, and advise suppliers and customers of the move, giving instructions regarding deliveries and returns (ideally deliveries to the old premises should cease several weeks prior to any move to minimise moving stocks of raw materials).

(f) Obtain TV licence if appropriate.

(g) Check location of photocopiers for access, control, and floor loading.

(h) Arrange refuse/waste disposal by authorised contractor.

(i) Assess equipment, furniture, fittings required – check delivery delays and order appropriately.

(j) Obtain at least two quotations for the actual move using specialist movers for safes, heavy machinery and equipment etc. Check insurance position re move.

(k) Give notice to terminate all service supplies on old site (or assign to new occupier – if possible) and set up such services for the new facility.

(l) Prepare data on building, services, for staff.

(m) Carry out a fire drill as soon as possible after occupation.

(n) Change locks once all fitting out work is completed.

(o) Preserve three sets of building and fitting out plans safely.

(p) Re-examine insurance cover.

(q) Check RATING valuation and claim for any period when, due to the fitting out works, a void rate benefit is obtainable.

(r) Once practical completion of fitting out works is certified by the building surveyor or architect, arrange for the preparation of a snagging list which the builder should complete within 14 or 21 days.

(s) Fix a date for the expiry of the defects liability period (usually six months for building works, 12 months for mechanical and electrical services after completion of the works).

Freehold

Introduction

Assuming there is a choice of buying or leasing a property, a decision regarding the most appropriate needs to be made. This choice will vary not only because of individual preferences but also on timing as much as any other factor. At one stage in an organisation's life it may be preferable to buy, at other times leasing may be more appropriate.

Speculation

Although there may be a temptation to use property for speculative purposes rather than simply as a means of housing the business itself, this may be best resisted unless a very clear view can be taken of the strategy and there is considerable and well-founded confidence concerning the long-term strength of property demand both generally and in the particular area.

Long-term lock-in

Buying a freehold could be actively contemplated in the following circumstances.

(a) When the long-term plans of the business call for it to be situated in a particular area for a considerable time.

(b) When the nature of the business is such that the means of production cannot be easily moved.

(c) When the business has, or has access to surplus funds which it is prepared to see tied up in property assets for a long period.

(d) When there is confidence that the underlying value of property in the area chosen will, at least, not depreciate.

(e) When there is a wish to be able to predict and control the cost of property occupation (this can be difficult with leasehold property as it is virtually impossible to predict rental increases).

(f) When there is a need to be able constantly to change the internal layout of the property to accommodate changes in working processes and practices (whilst this is possible with leased property, the approval of the landlord will constantly need to be sought and there will be pressure to agree to reinstatement undertakings thus leading to further costs on termination of occupation).

Using the investment

The value of the property acquired will form part of the assets of the business. Such value can be used to support the balance sheet or even used to generate cash at some time in the future by means of a sale and lease back arrangement. Alternatively, the value can be left out of the balance sheet, thus being available as a hidden reserve.

> *Note* Some companies (particularly listed PLCs) omit the market value of their freehold property assets from their balance sheets. Having available such 'hidden' assets may be advantageous at times of (for example) hostile takeover bids. Of course the original value of the property must be disclosed within the accounts, and anyone with details of the property portfolio may be able to make a reasoned assessment of the current value.

Seizing opportunities

Keeping a careful watch on the property market may enable an owner to take advantage of opportunities. Whilst dabbling in the property market may be a dilution of management attention from its core business, it may be possible to obtain additional profits as a result of such awareness. For example, acquiring adjoining properties may grant flexibility of use of the existing premises, but also the value of the two buildings in one ownership may be greater than the individual values. The potential of such MARRIAGES OF INTERESTS should not be overlooked.

Position

Property assets are unique in that they cannot be moved around as can most other assets. Whereas the original location may have been ideal for the business, circumstances tend to change and the original reasons may tend to disappear or even be replaced by pressures which might make a relocation necessary. Whereas to no small extent all property occupation other than a short-term licence tends to lock the occupier into a location, a freehold may tend to act as a greater 'anchor' simply because of the capital investment. Few businesses will wish to take too great a loss on a freehold investment particularly if its value appears in the balance sheet.

Use

Whilst to some extent the range of uses to which a freehold property can be put tends to be much greater than those allowed by a lease (particularly if there is a restricted user clause), the requirements of local planners may constrain the widest use of the premises.

Inelastic supply

Generally, property assets are an inelastic supply since each position is unique. If considering an investment when it is planned that the business will grow, consideration needs to be given to the possibility of acquiring land so that flexibility of use of any building(s) erected upon it can be obtained. If the original building erected upon the land is such that extension or additional bays can be added at will, this can help overcome the 'inelastic supply' nature of the location to a considerable extent.

Guarantees

> **Introduction**
>
> Smaller organisations or those without a long history of reasonable trading results may be requested, on entering into property commitments (e.g. a lease or licence), to supply the names of persons and/or organisations who are prepared to act as guarantors to the performance of the organisation of its financial obligations.

Directors as guarantors

Usually the guarantors requested by a landlord are the directors of the organisation. A guarantee is a legally enforceable personal undertaking and, if called upon, the guarantor must provide any shortfall (or a shortfall to the limit of the guarantee given). If the organisation gets into financial difficulties this undertaking could prove very costly and meeting the liability very difficult not least since, if the organisation is in trouble, the director may already be having difficulty obtaining his/her salary. Too often guarantees are given with insufficient consideration of the onerous liability being entered into.

Security

This situation may become even more serious if the guarantor is required to provide security, for example, their home. If unable to meet the debts they have guaranteed, the security pledged could then be seized by the creditor and sold as payment or part payment.

Minimising the effect

If the organisation needs the premises, there may be no option but to agree to provide personal guarantees. However, these should be limited either in amount or in time or both. Thus a director providing a guarantee might stipulate that the guarantee should be restricted to:

(a) (say) £10,000,

(b) the first three years of the term of the [lease],

(c) the payment of rent (only),

and be payable only provided the creditor has given official notice of [time] of their intent to call in the guarantee and allowed the guarantor(s) sufficient time to try to raise alternative funds to settle the outstanding payments.

In addition, the guarantor should endeavour to gain agreement to their guarantee ceasing on assignment (in which case the landlord will almost certainly require fresh replacement guarantors for any assignee).

Negotiation

Whilst there may be an understandable wish to minimise the effect of the guarantor, the interests of the landlord are diametrically opposed to this and there will need to be some negotiation to achieve a compromise acceptable to both parties.

Option

If open-ended guarantees are insisted on (i.e. they are not protected by any of the limitations set out above), it may be advisable to try to insert an OPTION TO BREAK the lease or licence after say five years. If this is agreed, then should the organisation get into difficulties, once again the effect is to limit the total amount of the personal guarantees provided. If there is an option it is essential to ensure that not only are the requirements to effect its exercise strictly adhered to but also all covenants are complied with.

Health and Safety

> **Introduction**
>
> With the advent of the 1993 workplace safety requirements, the UK version of the European Union's 'Safety in the Workplace' which came into force on 1 January 1993 with a staged effectiveness period ending in 1996, health and safety passed from being the responsibility of the personnel department to the property department – if not entirely then as a shared responsibility. The thrust of the directives is not merely compliance on the part of all property occupiers and employers but a need for action and to evidence such action at every workplace. Accordingly, that a record of data, implementation and updating should be kept at each workplace not least since the regulatory authorities will expect to see such documentation there.

The following policy/procedure envisages that at each workplace there will be a folder or wallet (which for the sake of convenience is referred to as 'Workplace Safety' hereafter). In that wallet should be kept (and kept updated) the various items set out below.

The legislation places a wide-ranging and onerous responsibility on every employer, and implementation of the requirements should be made the responsibility of a senior, even board level, manager in the organisation. A competent person should be retained to carry out safety and risk assessments. Competency is judged on training, experience and knowledge of the workplace and/or process (thus bridging the property administration, production and personnel disciplines).

A question-and-answer tactic has been adopted to demonstrate need for action.

A. HEALTH AND SAFETY POLICY

> <u>Note</u> This is not a new requirement, having first been required by the Health and Safety etc at Work Act 1974.

(a) Is there a Health and Safety Policy (see draft below)
available in all workplaces and to all employees? YES/NO

If YES, has it been updated following the introduction of
the 1993 legislation? YES/NO

If NO, ensure updated policy is devised and
(if YES or NO) is incorporated in Workplace
Safety. Date (when completed) ....

(b) Has the policy been brought to attention of all employees? YES/NO

If, YES, set review date to incorporate new policy. Date set ....

If NO, set date to do so. Date done................

DRAFT HEALTH & SAFETY POLICY

1. AIMS

(a) To ensure, as far as is reasonably practicable, the health and safety of all employees whilst at work.

(b) To comply with all relevant health and safety legislation, regulations and codes of practice.

(c) To provide safe and healthy conditions of work, plant and systems.

2. RESPONSIBILITIES

The company
(i) To work towards the achievement of these policy aims.

(ii) To provide appropriate training, advice, protective clothing, equipment and documentation as is necessary or advisable.

(iii) To carry out an assessment of risks and endeavour to reduce or eliminate these.

(iv) To provide written systems of work for all and any procedures which are exposed to hazard.

(v) To record notification of hazards and accidents and incorporate improvements suggested as a result of investigations conducted following such notifications as soon as possible.

Managers and supervisors
(i) To be responsible for the execution of the safety policy as far as the department/employees for which he/she is responsible.

(ii) To be responsible, as far as reasonably practicable, for the safety of all persons working in or visiting his/her department, and for all plant/equipment under his/her control.

(iii) To ensure, in the event of accident, that prompt and appropriate first aid is administered, that further medical assistance is obtained if necessary, that the circumstances of the incident are investigated and reported on, and that recommendations made as a result of an investigation are implemented.

(iv) To ensure the Workplace Safety folder is kept and displayed, that its contents are brought to the attention of every employee, and that all employees are conversant with such data.

(v) To ensure protective clothing/equipment is used at all times where and when necessary.

(vi) To ensure that employees are conversant with the accident/hazard reporting procedure and that notification of Hazards is passed to the appropriate person for action.

Employees
(i) To make themselves familiar with and adhere to safety procedures, including the fire alarm procedure and evacuation route(s).

(ii) To wear protective clothing/equipment at all times as and when necessary, and to report any defects in such clothing/equipment to their supervisor.

(iii) To report all accidents/incidents to a supervisor, and to carry out instructions given by a supervisor.

(iv) To report all safety and health hazards and machinery defects using the hazard report procedure.

(v) To cooperate with the organisation at all times on matters of safety.

Safety representatives
(i) To assist the employer (and employees) in the assessment and reduction of risk and hazards, by being aware of the implementation and effect of procedures and work in the workplace.

(ii) To advise the employer on matters of concern raised by employees and liaise/help in implementing them where possible/practicable.

(iii) As a member of the Safety Committee to take full part in its deliberations and operations.

Safety Committee (if applicable)

(i) To further the interest of all involved in the reduction and/or elimination of risk, or, failing this, of its control.

(ii) To advise management on safety matters.

(iii) To assist in the education of employees in operating safe working practices.

(iv) To raise awareness of the need for high-profile safety policy/procedure.

3. ADMINISTRATION

The Safety Officer is [name], Deputy [name], and is responsible for:

(i) preparing, reviewing and updating this Policy, accident/hazard reporting procedures, fire and safety procedures and evacuation guidance

(ii) accepting and actioning accident/hazard report forms

(iii) ensuring compliance with the responsibilities laid down in this policy statement and reporting failure to comply to senior management for sanctions to be applied

(iv) liaison with health and safety officers, insurers, factory and environmental health officers, Fire Service, etc., and ensuring appropriate recommendations are effected

(v) implementing the requirements of the Reporting of Injuries, Diseases and Dangerous Occurrences Regulations 1995 (RIDDOR) and all such other legislation or requirements as may be enacted from time to time.

Signed .... Managing Director......................Safety Officer

Date of issue .... To be reviewed on ....[date]

B. RISK AND HAZARD ASSESSMENT

A competent person must be appointed to carry out safety and risk assessments. Competency is judged on training, experience, knowledge or other qualities. The legislation requires detailed, and ongoing, assessments of risks and hazards to be made *at each and every location*.

RISK REVIEW/ASSESSMENT

Employers have been required to assess risk in and arising from the

HEALTH AND SAFETY

workplace comprehensively with effect from January 1993. The answers to these questions must be sought and assessment made of *all* hazards at individual locations. Following this, measures taken as a result of the identification of the hazard must be noted.

(a) Is there a fire escape/precautions procedure? YES/NO

If NO, prepare one. When prepared, this should form part of Workplace Safety. Date completed ....

Such a procedure should state the person with deputies responsible for ensuring evacuation of the workplace in the event of serious and imminent danger. Date completed ....

(b) Are all staff aware of fire procedure and precautions? YES/NO

If NO, make them aware and insert date completed in Workplace Safety Date completed ....

(c) Are there any areas in the workplace from which there is only one exit? YES/NO

If YES, consider whether an alternative exit (even where this involves a right of way over adjoining property) is possible. If this is not possible, make staff aware of the dangers of these areas and consider an alternative action that can be taken to minimise risk. Note date of advice to staff and alternative actions in Workplace Safety.
Date completed ....

(d) Is there a fire alarm? YES/NO

If YES, ensure that those present are familiar with it, that it is tested regularly and insert date of most recent test (or regular timing of tests) in Workplace Safety.

If NO, what alternative method(s) are used to alert those present?

....

(e) Is there a plan of the premises showing all exits, and all hazards which could impede escape and/or cause harm? YES/NO

If NO, prepare one and place a copy with Workplace Safety. Incorporate with such data any specific requirements made as a result of the issue of a Fire Certificate, responsibility for ensuring fire escapes and exits are clear and unlocked when premises are in use, etc.

Hazard assessment completed ....

Note *The hazards covered by this question are all-embracing. They would include all machinery and plant, guillotines, water heaters, all electrical equipment and supplies, geysers, unlighted stairs, low ceilings, steps that are awkward to traverse, as well as the more obvious items such as chemicals, vehicle movements, fire, etc. These items are included for illustration only and are not exhaustive. Individual workplace assessments must be completed for every hazard. All hazards identified should be listed and dealt with as shown below.*

(f) Is firefighting equipment available? YES/NO

If YES, ensure staff are trained in its use, and that the equipment is maintained and checked regularly.

If NO, arrange to install fire fighting equipment at least to the standard required by the Fire Officer.

(g) Is there a necessity to bring fire and other risks to the attention of visitors/contractors on the premises? YES/NO

If YES, ensure an adequate procedure is devised, brought to the attention of those visiting the premises and that adherence to the requirements is ensured during such visits. Note the person responsible for this in Workplace Safety.

WARNING This section might need rewording once the Fire Precautions (Places of Work) Regulations 1992 are brought into operation.

C. HAZARD IDENTIFICATION/CONTROL/REDUCTION/ELIMINATION

(a) All employees will be and are encouraged to make [a named employee] aware of all hazards to ensure their consideration, reduction or elimination, by means of the hazard report form, a supply of which is in Workplace Safety.

Staff informed ....

(b) For each hazard identified, a procedure to minimise accident or harm resulting from it, any possible manner of elimination, timing of elimination, etc., must by compiled and incorporated as part of Workplace Safety.

Procedures compiled ....

(c) The name and position of the person in the company responsible for the execution of health and safety matters must be stated in Workplace

HEALTH AND SAFETY

Safety with the name and position of the person responsible at the workplace. Date completed ....

(d) Have all staff been informed of potential hazards and the methods for coping with or reducing them, and are they regularly reminded of this? YES/NO
If YES, state date of latest reminder in Workplace Safety.
Date ....

If NO, – carry out information exercise.

(e) Have employees been instructed that, unless their work or duties specifically require them to do so they should not attempt to repair or alter any machinery, fitting or fitment, etc., and should bring any defect in such items to the attention of the person responsible for safety at the workplace to retain suitably trained and competent workers to effect adequate repairs?
YES/NO
If YES, state date in Workplace Safety. Date ....

If NO, ensure such instructions are issued and confirm date.

Note   It may be advisable to state this restriction in the contract of employment.

Date effected ....

Where regular dates for inspection/maintenance of equipment are set, confirm such dates in Workplace Safety. Where there are no regular dates, insert a date on which the possibility of maintenance should be considered.

D. HEALTH PROTECTION/SURVEILLANCE

(a) Is the work, working practice or environment likely to cause a work-related disease? YES/NO

If YES, identify technique(s)/procedure(s) to be used to identify such disease, its treatment, reduction of risk, and list details in Workplace Safety. Date listed ....

b) Are display screens in use?

If YES, have all workstations been considered to ensure the desk, chair, screen, etc., are arranged in accordance with legal requirements? YES/NO

For employees who use display screens for a substantial period of time it is necessary to arrange suitable breaks from screen work (say five minutes every hour) for work of a different nature (not necessarily a rest break). Screens also need to be checked to ensure glare is reduced/eliminated and sight tests provided or paid for.

E. MANUAL HANDLING

Are employees required to carry out manual handling operations (i.e. to lift or move heavy or bulky objects) in the course of their employment? YES/NO

If YES, do such objects weigh in excess of 56lb, or, if less, are they required to be stacked above head height, where the act of stacking or moving could cause strain? YES/NO

If YES, outline steps taken to provide alternative means of lifting and/or to minimise danger from such lifting in Workplace Safety.

F. PROTECTIVE EQUIPMENT/CLOTHING

Is protective equipment or clothing (overalls, protective shoes, earplugs, gloves, etc.) required for working? YES/NO

If YES, ensure the items provided are adequate for the purpose required, that they are regularly maintained, and replaced whenever necessary.

G. WORKING PRACTICES

Are safety matters considered whenever procedures or practices are introduced or changed? YES/NO

If NO, ensure that this occurs as routine.

HEALTH AND SAFETY

WORKPLACE SAFETY – THE FOLDER

In a clear plastic A4 wallet, itemise the contents of the workplace safety folder. These should include safety and first aid policies (and date of last issue); fire escape precautions procedure (also posted on fire exit routes and by fire alarms); hazards in the workplace – assessments, list, plan, procedures and risk prevention data; accident/hazard report forms; reminder diary; and the names of the persons responsible for safety.

Accident and Hazard reporting procedure

[Name of organisation] wishes to hear swiftly of all hazards or potential hazards occurring in the course of its operations. To do this it has devised hazard reports (supply in this wallet) which should be completed by any employee becoming aware of a hazard. This form is to be passed to the person responsible for safety in the workplace and by them, to the person responsible in the organisation.

This form should also be used to confirm details of all accidents which may need to be reported under the Reporting of Injuries, Diseases, and Dangerous Occurrences Regulations 1995 and/or recorded in Accident Book B1510.

Diary

Staff reminded of fire procedure precautions	Date ....
Most recent fire drill (check Fire Certificate for obligations for frequency – usually twice yearly)	....
Staff reminded of danger areas	....
Staff reminded of hazard coping/reducing procedure	....
Staff reminded not to tamper with machinery, etc.	....
Equipment inspection dates	Item ....
	Item ....
	Item ....

Insurance

Introduction

Whilst in larger organisations the function of insurance tends to be separated from that of the property administrator, in many cases the responsibilities are either dealt with as a combined function or else the departments need to work in close harmony as so many of the risks requiring consideration are related to or result from the occupation of property. Where leasehold property is occupied, the range of covers to be effected may be laid down by the lease and the obligation of the lessee is merely to reimburse the landlord for the costs incurred in effecting the required covers. In this instance the occupier's input may be restricted to ensuring the cover is accurate and the sum demanded is fair (see below). However, where freehold property is owned a more proactive attitude needs to be adopted.

Guidance to insurance covers is outside the scope of this book (although the subject of a future title in this series) and this section seeks only to highlight the administrative items which may be the responsibility of the property administrator.

Freehold portfolio

From the time of *exchange* of contracts (i.e. not completion) for the purchase of a freehold property, the organisation should ensure that adequate insurance cover is effected for the property. The extent of the cover is for individual organisations to determine but essentially the property should be insured against fire and an associated range of risks – impact, explosion, riot, etc. The sums insured should also be revisited annually to ensure adequacy bearing in mind the implications of 'average' should there be underinsurance. The basis of insurance (e.g. reinstatement or 'new for old') should be considered as this may well affect the determination of the sums insured.

If the determination of the covers is left to the property administrator and he or she is not experienced in insurance, it may be helpful to retain a broker who has experience of the industry in which the organisation is engaged. Such appointment should be made on a fee basis with the broker remitting any commission earned to the organisation so that the range of duties to be performed by the broker can be compared with the costs involved.

Leasehold occupation

As stated above, normally the landlord will insure and recharge the lessee for the range of covers stipulated in the lease. Any reduction in this range of covers needs to be negotiated when the lease is effected. This places the lessee in a somewhat invidious position since they may have little say over the costs involved particularly since it was stated in the case of *Havenbridge v Boston Dyers Ltd* that the landlord is under no obligation to shop around to obtain the lowest premium. With a full repairing lease it is prudent to request that the interest of the lessee is noted on the policy of the landlord. In the event of any underinsurance the landlord will be precluded from trying to pass on to the lessee the responsibility for any shortfall. The following draft letter could be used

---

Dear [name of landlord]

Address of property   Details of lease

As you are aware we are your lessees/lessees of your clients at the above property.

Included in the landlord's covenants is an obligation to insure the property, whilst included in the tenant's covenants is an obligation to refund the costs of this insurance premium.

I should be obliged if you would confirm that this company's interest as tenant under the above lease is included on the policy.

If this is not the case please take this as our request to ensure that our interest is noted immediately. Your acknowledgement of this request and confirmation that this has been effected would be appreciated, but if we do not hear from you [or your client] we will assume our interest is noted.

Yours faithfully/sincerely

Note Such a letter could be sent stapled to the cheque in payment of rent and/or premium or else sent by recorded delivery so that its non-receipt is difficult to contend.

INSURANCE

Advice of incidents

Not all incidents that occur at working premises will be covered by insurance. However, the property administrator may wish to know of all incidents whether claimable or not. If there is a risk management process to help determine whether or not losses should be covered by insurance or not, then records of all incidents will be required. The following draft incident folder could be kept at each location and will then provide the person on the spot with details of what needs to be done in each case.

Organisations will need to make an employee responsible for incident reporting at each site, and every supervisor and manager should be encouraged to remember to advise that person so that proper record is made of every incident.

For organisations that do not have an administration manual or similar instruction book in which the procedure to be followed in the event of incidents can be set out, a general incident folder may provide the essential aide-memoire to line/local management for the reporting of both safety hazards and incidents.

Concept

An A4 plastic folder containing a number of forms for immediate use in the event of an incident, held by the local manager/employee appointed to report all incidents to the property/insurance administrator.

Contents

(a) Procedures to be followed

(b) Incident forms

(c) Hazard forms (if hazard reporting of safety matters is to be made via the same procedure)

(d) Panic numbers (for management contacts to be advised out of office hours)

(e) Telephone hotline procedure

(f) Incident checklists

(g) Pre-addressed internal/external envelopes

(h) Contents re-order slip

(i) Check sheet for 'correspondent' to note action taken and dates, etc.

> *Note* It may also be prudent for each correspondent to have or have access to a cheap camera, and to be instructed to take photos of every incident.

Procedure

1. Note date, time and report source on Incident form.
2. Visit site of incident and record as much information as possible.
3. If you have access to a camera, take several photos particularly endeavouring to obtain views from different angles. If no camera is available, make a sketch of the scene of the incident, including on it all relevant data.
4. Collate the names of all present and involved.
5. Should the incident involve physical injury to any person, or be such that it appears to involve loss or damage to company property in excess of [£5000], use the telephone hotline to advise (contact). If the incident occurs out of normal office hours, use the Panic number list to advise [contact].
6. Follow any instructions issued by [contact].
7. Request statements from willing eyewitnesses and any others involved.

WARNING Advice should be taken before witness statements are compiled as they could be subject to legal disclosure requirements.

8. Complete the other information required on the incident form.
9. Review the information obtained and witness statements taken to ensure that there is, on paper, a realistic resume of the events and the incident, such that a third party reviewing the data at a much later date will be able to gain an accurate insight into the occurrence.
10. If the incident is such that a claims checklist is applicable advise those included on the checklist to commence sourcing the information required.
11. Send the incident form with all ancillary items, including jottings, witness statements, sketches, etc., to the contact within 12 hours of the incident. Follow this initial notification with any supplementary information, photos, claim checklists data, etc., as soon as possible.
12. React to, and obtain further information requested by contact and the insurers as requested, assisting with any inspection and subsequent investigation.

INSURANCE

> *Note* It is good policy, even if the telephone hotline is used, to obtain some written record from the correspondent – initial jottings may be of assistance to an incident investigator and thus should be passed through to the contact.

Incident form

An incident form (draft below) could be used to ensure prompt notification of incidents.

URGENT

Please complete as soon as possible and send immediately to contact in the event of any injury to personnel, or contact – in the event of any damage or loss to property, or products, etc.

Dept/Shop/Site .... Date ....

Report completed by .... Position ....

Telephone ....

Details of occurrence ....

....

....

....

Time of incident .... Police informed ....

If police informed, details of station/officer ....

....

....

Witness details ....

....

Organisation contact for further details ....

Other back-up documentation (attached/to follow) Specify ....

....

....

Office use only

Claimable?   YES/NO   If YES, which policy ....

Reportable?   YES/NO   If YES, entered in Accident Book? ....

Date claim/report made ....

Contact numbers

Large or multi-facility organisations may need to develop a list of names and telephone numbers for each site, or division, etc. If contingency/disaster planning is in operation this list could form the initial part of such planning, i.e. swift reporting of the incident.

Out-of-hours-contacts

In all cases of loss, fire or other serious incident out of normal hours where there is injury to an individual or the potential loss seems likely to exceed £5000, telephone:

Manufacturing

Works Director	Tel ....
Property Administrator	Tel ....
Works Manager	Tel ....
Chief Engineer	Tel ....
Company Secretary ⎫ (for insurers)	Tel ....
Insurance Manager ⎭	Tel ....
Chief Executive	Tel ....
Safety Officer	Tel ....
Personnel Officer	Tel ....
Shift Managers	Tel ....
Transport Manager	Tel ....
Purchasing	Tel ....
etc.	

Retailing

Area Controller
Property Administrator
Area Manager
Company Secretary ⎫ (for insurers)
Insurance Manager ⎭
Chief Executive
Personnel Officer
Transport Manager
Warehouse Manager
Buyer
etc.

INSURANCE

Telephone hotline

A 'hotline' can be used (linked for out-of-hours calls to an answerphone) if there is difficulty obtaining written information from correspondents. Using this facility they can 'notify' by means of a swift telephone call.

Correspondents should be prepared when the message ends to provide the following data in this set order.

1. Date of incident.
2. Time of incident.
3. Name of correspondent.
4. Site of incident.
5. Brief description of incident.
6. Injury caused (names and apparent injuries sustained).
7. Damage caused (details of damage with approximate value).
8. Likely length of interruption to production (if any).
9. Action being taken (including using the panic number system).
10. Telephone number of correspondent or person dealing with the incident.

To ensure record is complete each item should be prefaced by stating its reference number as above, e.g. state 'One – 28 July 1997, Two – 19.45, Three – Frank Jones, Four – paint works, Birmingham . . .' and so on. If an item is not applicable, its number should be stated followed by the words 'Not applicable'.

>Note   An internal E-mail system provides a further alternative means of notification.

Claim checklists

Claim checklists are lists of the information and data that will be required by the insurers before they can start processing a claim. The list should be agreed for each cover at renewal. Each correspondent can then be advised of the requirements in each instance. In this way without reference to, or being chased by, the contact he or she knows what information needs to be sourced and submitted. Examples of claim checklists are given below.

ONE STOP PROPERTY

1) Retail stock and/or cash loss

Item required	Person responsible
Incident form	Shop Manager
Till check and cross check	Area staff
Stock check	Area staff
Shop staff statements	Area staff
Managers statement	Area staff
Police details	Area Manager
Description of suspect	Area staff
Prior till / stock checks	Office Manager
Any disciplinary letters issued	Office/Personnel Manager
Staff records	Office/Personnel Manager
Shop incident history (if any)	Office/Personnel Manager

2) Fire

Item required	Person responsible
Incident form	Manager
Stock/Product/Machinery/Plant loss	Manager/Accounts
Valuation of Stock, etc., loss	Accounts/Auditors
Loss estimate	Accounts/Auditors
General information	Insurance Manager
Photos	Insurance Manager
Builders repair estimate	Manager/Engineer
Incident history	Office Manger
Replacement lead times	Purchasing Dept.

Internal Rents

Introduction

An organisation which trades from both freehold and leasehold properties may find it difficult to compare the results of units in such properties unless it levies those occupying freehold sites with the equivalent of the rental charges that are borne by leasehold sites. To deal with this problem many such organisations set up a process of calculating and charging 'internal rents'.

Assessing the charge

To some extent, whichever way the charge is calculated is irrelevant since what is important is that some equality of treatment of profit centres is provided. However, linking the calculation to the value of the property generated by VALUATION is perhaps the most logical. If a percentage of this value is used, such a figure can be revised each time the property is valued thus providing a regular increase in the charge similar to what happens each time a rent is reviewed.

Alternatively, an assessment of the likely rent for each property can be arrived at by referring to the rents being borne by surrounding leasehold properties.

Whichever method is chosen it needs to be both logical and sustainable so that it is accepted as a fair charge by those responsible for the profit-earning capacity of the units.

Accounting

Those organisations which operate such a system tend to set up a 'property division' or subsidiary which generates the rental charge on the trading units. The income can be used by the property division to acquire and/or develop other properties some of which may have occupiers from outside the organisation. The advantage of a division becoming responsible for the properties of an organisation may be that it operates a regular maintenance and repair programme (the resulting costs of which may also be chargeable against the operating units as they would under a lease. In addition, specialist attention to property may generate opportunities for OBTAINING VALUE.

Landlord and Tenant Act

Introduction

The main thrust of the Landlord and Tenant Act 1954 is to attempt to protect lessees from excessively aggressive landlords and particularly to protect their positions in the event of the lease under which they occupy the property coming to an end and the landlord seeking to regain occupation. The reason for this protective approach is the recognition that by its occupation the lessee may have increased the value and/or appeal of the property and may also have more to lose (i.e. their business in a particular location) than mere occupation rights should the lease, on expiry, not be renewed.

WARNING The provisions of the Landlord and Tenant Act are complicated and specific advice should be taken from an appropriate source before taking action or responding to action under the Act. These notes provide outline guidance only.

Termination of lease

Whilst a lease will be expected to come to an end at the conclusion of its term, this will actually only occur if the landlord takes the required steps under the Act. The required action is set out below.

(a) Not more than 12 nor less than 6 months before the termination date, the landlord is required to serve a notice (known as a section 25 notice) on the lessee (tenant) terminating the lease on the expiry date. Normally it will be stated that the landlord does not oppose the grant of a new tenancy to the lessee. The notice will state the requirements sent out in b) and c) below.

(b) Within two months of the date of the Section 25 notice the lessee must reply indicating whether or not he requires a new tenancy.

(c) Assuming the lessee does want a new tenancy he must also apply to the court not earlier than two months after the date of the section 25 notice (and not later than four months after that date).

Late notice

If the landlord is late serving the original notice then the lease is regarded as being extended (or 'held over') until the date that the Section 25 notice becomes effective (i.e. its own date plus six months).

Opposition to new lease

However, a landlord can oppose the grant of a new lease. The grounds for such opposition are as follows.

(a) The landlord wishes to:

    (i) redevelop or reconstruct the premises.

    (ii) use the premises for his own purposes, or,

    (iii) convert the premises (previously let in parts one of which was to the lessee) so that it can be let as a single entity because he will be able to maximise the return in this way.

(b) The landlord wishes to oppose the lessee renewing the occupation because the lessee:

    (i) is in breach of the repairing covenants of the lease,

    (ii) has persistently paid the rent late,

    (iii) is in breach of other substantial obligations under the lease,

(c) The landlord wishes to offer the lessee suitable alternative premises.

In these instances the landlord may be able to bring the lease to an end on the termination date of the Section 25 notice and the lessee will not be able to obtain a new lease. The landlord may be required to prove the reason for the non-renewal. Thus, if he states that he intends redeveloping the site, he will be required to produce plans of the redevelopment, planning approval, etc. to the court.

If the renewal is successfully opposed because of the items listed under a) above, the landlord will also be liable to pay the lessee compensation for the non-renewal. However this compensation is only equal to the rateable value of the property where the premises have been occupied for 14 years and twice that value where the premises have been occupied for longer than 14 years.

Court-determined lease

Normally once the Section 25 notice has been served, and assuming a new tenancy is required by both parties, the two parties will attempt to agree terms for the new term. If this is the case any court proceedings actioned by the lessee as a protection will be discontinued and a new lease will be agreed and become effective from the expiry of the old lease (or six months after the date of the Section 25 notice if it was served late).

Agreeing terms for a new lease is not always possible, however, and sometimes there is a need to refer to the court for determination.

If suitably acceptable terms for a new lease cannot be agreed, or the lessee successfully resists the landlord's efforts not to renew the lease, the court may decide on the terms of the new lease which cannot be for a term in excess of 14 years. In such a case, most of the covenants in the old lease will simply be repeated in the new lease. A modern review pattern may be inserted if the expiring lease was on an outdated pattern (e.g. 21 or 42 years) and the rent will be decided by a judge with the assistance of an expert witness.

Tenancies outside the Act

The Landlord and Tenant Acts were enacted to protect lessees or tenants. If the parties agree that an occupation will be outside the scope of the Act (i.e. that the protections under the Act should not be applicable) then they need to apply to the Court for permission to enter into such an agreement and for that permission to be evidenced (refer to PRIVITY OF CONTRACT).

Leasehold

Introduction

Prospective lessees do not always realise how onerous the obligations included in a lease can be. Since such obligations (COVENANTS) can rarely be altered once the lease is signed and, in most cases, the balance of power is in favour of the landlord, these points require careful attention during the negotiations – the only time when the parties may actually negotiate on something approaching an equal basis. The bias of power in favour of the landlord should not be underestimated by the lessee. In negotiating a lease the items in the following checklist should be considered well before the commitment is entered into.

Checklist

1. Suggest restricting term to 15 years in order to protect occupation for a reasonable time yet minimise commitment. Leases effected for the last 30 years or so have tended to have terms of 25 years, but few businesses plan 25 years ahead. A shorter term may be more appropriate.

2. Resist the provision of sureties and/or personal GUARANTEES from directors or owners. For a director-owned limited liability company this negates the protection of the limited liability status. If the provision of guarantees is inevitable, restrict their time span.

3. Insist on a full structural survey before commitment and take necessary steps as result of such survey. Insert a SCHEDULE OF CONDITION in the lease to minimise exposure to repairing liabilities where the property is in poor repair.

4. Itemise any inherent defects and clarify obligations.

5. Resist the imposition of rent reviews at a greater frequency than five years – such a period is normally fair to both parties. During the property boom four and three year reviews were introduced (and still exist in some areas in the UK).

6. Resist upwards-only rent review clauses. The assumption that rent must always increase is fallacious. In times of recession (and, particularly

where an area suffers change), new rents fall and old rents need flexibility to be adjusted to match the market rent.

7. Avoid penal interest charges on late agreement of rent review. This is particularly iniquitous if the delay is the responsibility of the landlord.

8. Record rent review agreements using an agreed simple memorandum to avoid having to pay legal costs at each review.

9. If upwards only rent review is deleted suggest incorporating a provision to allow the lessee to initiate a review. In this way should rents fall and the landlord ignore the rent review process in the awareness that the rent could be reduced, the lessee can start the process to gain the lower rent.

10. Stipulate rent review dispute recourse is to expert not arbitrator. Whereas an arbitrator may tend to split the difference between the two parties (albeit having reviewed the evidence put before him/her by the parties), the expert should take account of the realities of the property situation by virtue of their own individual knowledge of the area.

11. Request that the expert should be knowledgeable of property but not necessarily a surveyor. It is arguable that the ultimate decision regarding rents should not be left to members of a profession whose increase in income is partly dependent on rents themselves increasing.

12. Avoid rent review confidentiality clauses. More open rental agreements should make the property market reflect real demand and values.

13. Try to delete the covenant requiring the lessee to keep the premises open. If the premises are loss-making it may save money to close them. This cannot be done with the usual clause requiring that the premises be kept open.

14. If there is a user clause ensure such restriction is not to be ignored in review. If the use is restrictive, this should affect the rental value, particularly at review.

15. If there is no need to have a wide or wider user clause (or permission for it to be extended), delete such a clause. The ability to widen the user clause can increase the rental value on review.

16. Resist time limits for agreement of rent reviews – the approach of deadlines can place undue pressure on the lessee.

17. Stipulate that there should be no contingent liability on assignment, or restrict it to initial assignee failure only. This minimises the exposure to the one assignee over whom the lessee has some control.

> *Note* With effect from 1 January 1996 this 'PRIVITY OF CONTRACT' obligation was made illegal for leases entered into after that date, although of course it still applies during the currency of leases effected prior to that date.

18. If removing the PRIVITY OF CONTRACT requirement (which could be described as a contingent liability clause) is resisted, try to agree a maximum financial liability to be met by the lessee in the event of an assignee failing.

19. If contingent liability is included, insist on right to underlet. (If an assignee fails, the assigning lessee collects the liability for the lease obligations but no rights of re-entry. However, in the event of any failure of an underlessee the original lessee can re-enter and re-occupy the premises and will be able to re-market the property.)

20. Include permission to underlet and assign subject only to landlord's consent 'not to be unreasonably withheld'. Flexibility in dealing with the property, particularly with a long lease, is essential.

21. Ensure, if there are service charges, that these are independently audited and that the proportion applicable is set out clearly – to minimise the possibility of overcharging.

22. Ensure that any shortfall due to other lessees not paying their proportion of any service charge is not to be shared by the remaining lessees.

23. Insert a lessee's right to insure, or at least obtain alternative insurance quote, to minimise financial exposure because of landlord's record which may be based on other properties and/or factors outside lessee's control.

24. Insert right of lessee's interest to be endorsed on insurance policy to minimise exposure if landlord has underinsured. A further alternative is to ensure word 'reasonable' precedes 'insurance premiums' in the lease. At least this should ensure that a competitive premium is paid and recharged. (But note *Havenbridge Ltd v Boston Dyers Ltd* case ruling in which landlord was found to have no obligation to find cheapest quote.)

25. Remove all COVENANTS and any restrictions which could impair the operation of the business of the lessee.

Lessee's works

> **Introduction**
>
> There are three reasons for lessees carrying out work to the premises they occupy under the terms of their lease. These are:
>
> a) because they are required to do so by statute or regulation.
>
> b) because they wish to customise the premises for their own occupation.
>
> c) because they are required to perform such works by the landlord to bring the premises to the level of repair and redecoration required under the lease (see SCHEDULE OF DILAPIDATIONS).

Statutory requirement

If work is required to be carried out in order for premises to be fit places for work to be conducted (for example, where employees can work safely, etc.), most leases will allocate to the lessee the responsibility for carrying out such works and for paying for them. If the lease is silent on this point then the landlord may well be liable although it may be convenient for the lessee to arrange for the works to be carried out (at the landlord's expense) merely so that the works can be planned round working requirements.

It is likely that, when the Fire Precautions (Places of Work) Regulations 1992 are enacted, that this could involve such work. These regulations require occupiers to be proactive rather than reactive.

Customising premises

Carrying out such building works or alterations in order to make them more appropriate to the work requirements throws up a number of problems, namely:

(a) a requirement for permissions from landlord, building regulations and Fire Officer.

(b) the question of payment for the works.

(c) the problem of the relationship of such works with the rest of the premises.

Landlord's permission

Virtually all works, other than the most minor works, require the landlord's permission. This may be obtained by the landlord signing the plans and specification or it may require a full legal Licence for Alterations. It may be that the landlord is content for the works to be carried out as they enhance the value of the property. However, it is more likely that the landlord will insist on an undertaking from the lessee to reinstate the premises (to the state they were before the works were carried out).

Payment

The question of who is to fund the works must also be addressed. In many ways it may be simpler for the landlord to fund the works (which then pass into the landlord's ownership) and to recover the investment by increasing the rent. This may be feasible with some properties but may cause difficulties where the rent (inflated by the cost of the additions) is substantially more than the rent being paid in respect of similar properties in the area. One way of achieving this is to leave the rent as it is and by separate letter of agreement for the lessee to undertake to pay an agreed sum in respect of the added investment made by the landlord on their behalf.

The alternative method of payment is for the works to be funded by the lessee. If this occurs then arrangements should be made to exclude the value of the works from the next one or two (or more) rent reviews otherwise the lessee will be in the position of paying for the works and then paying additional rent for the benefit of an extension or renovation, etc. that he has funded. In addition, at the termination of the lease he may be obliged to remove the works and make good the premises.

Great care should be taken in recording the intentions of the parties in this regard. Not only does there need to be a form of words stating that the effect of the works will be ignored at the next [number] reviews, but also any clause in the RENT REVIEW arrangements which enables the landlord to bring such works into the calculation needs to be specifically excluded.

Minor works

It may be possible to effect minor works without formal permission. However, care should be taken to determine whose property such works become. Generally if the works are fixed to the structure then they are usually regarded as becoming part of the landlord's fixtures, if removable then they usually remain the lessee's property. The question of responsibility for insuring such items also needs to be ascertained.

Licence

Introduction

Whilst most occupations of business premises are on a freehold or leasehold basis some organisations have developed a policy of avoiding the longer-term commitment that tends to be associated with both those forms of occupation, preferring instead to take a short-term licence.

Status

A licence grants to the licensee the right to occupy the premises in accordance with its terms for the period stated. Licences are granted outside the protection of the LANDLORD AND TENANT ACT and thus convey none of the protections regarding renewal of the lease on expiry. Legal advice should be sought to ensure the licence is truly, in law, a licence rather than a business tenancy.

Use

For businesses with few 'non-human' assets (i.e. organisations which are people-based) taking short-term licences can have considerable attraction since landlords may be happy to grant short-term occupation at a concessionary rent whilst they either wait for other leases in a multi-occupation building to terminate, or for the property market to regain buoyancy before granting long-term occupancy rights and so on. It is better for property to be occupied than to remain empty since this both prevents severe deterioration and provides an income. Some organisations state they prefer to keep moving every few years since not only do they benefit from lower occupancy costs but also the concentration on relocation forces them to keep files slim and procedures efficient. Conversely, whoever is responsible for obtaining property has a constant challenge of finding suitable premises on a short-term basis.

Long-Term Planning

Introduction

If property assets are to be used in the most cost-effective way, the long-term premises requirements of the organisation need to be planned so that sufficient (and no more) space is available as and when required. There may be as much a need to ensure that surplus space is disposed of (or turned by means of letting or underletting into a revenue-producing asset) as there is to ensure that new space comes 'onstream' at the right time.

Preparing a plan

A premises plan needs to be prepared for at least the term covered by the long-term plan for the business of the organisation. If the business plan is restricted in time there may need to be separate consideration of the likely term/space required in view of the long-term nature of the property commitment. Although the property administrator should be involved in the preparation and refinement of the plan, the overall strategy needs to be determined at board (or equivalent) level. It should also be realised that the plan needs to be constantly updated, i.e. the premises plan should be updated each time the business plan is updated.

Plan content

A premises requirement plan should encompass the following data.

> *Note* It should not be overlooked that simply setting out the facts, and backing the facts with the PROPERTY REGISTER data, may generate the necessary decisions.

(a) Space required (projected on a time basis and compared with space available). This requirement is easy to state but may be anything but easy to achieve, particularly as it is ongoing and changing. In this respect, the best advice may be that if the organisation cannot project long-term then it may be better not to commit long-term. This may result in slightly higher occupation costs but at least all options (and all occupations) will be kept flexible.

Space required should be calculated

(i) on an absolute minimum basis – i.e. those pressing for space must be made to tailor their demands to the minimum.

(ii) in accordance with particular use – office, storage, production, retail, etc.

(iii) in accordance with time (possibly on an incremental basis).

All too often the automatic reaction to a space requirement is to make a long-term commitment for the maximum need when a time analysis will determine that short-term additional facilities supplementing a smaller long-term commitment would have been a better alternative.

(b) Location costs of current or alternative facilities – projected for the duration of the business plan or budget. Occupation is nearly always costly and these costs (most of which are, to a large extent, fixed and tend to rise and fall in accordance with the overall property market, may be unmarketable other than at a loss) need to be built into budgets, etc. and constantly re-examined in case savings can be made.

(c) Personnel and the projected ease of recruiting required labour in location, and of ease of manoeuvring raw materials and finished product. If the terms of trade of either or both have moved – or are projected to move against the organisation, then the planner needs to consider whether it is more economic to continue to use existing premises or to attempt to relocate (in which case the comparison of existing and alternative premises costs referred to in (b) above becomes more relevant.

(d) Any external factors likely to affect current location on a business-specific basis need to be identified in case these either reinforce a decision to stay or prompt consideration of a move. These factors could include technological change, market demand change, materials change, environmental pressures, political pressures, social pressures, etc.

(e) Position. Organisations move on average every 12 years. One should expect that with a business plan lasting say 15 years (five years detailed, five years in outline and five years in general intent), the possibility of a move might be required particularly since the rate of change of production methods, raw materials, and market demand is on the increase in most businesses.

(f) Cost incurred and the value invested in property assets to ensure that their value is maximised.

LONG-TERM PLANNING

> *Note*   *Regular VALUATIONS of property assets (even perhaps including leasehold interests) should be undertaken to enable objective decisions to be made regarding their continued use in the business.*

(g) As a further dimension, the value contained in property assets could be assessed for consideration as possible security to generate funds for use in the business, or, at times of high interest rates, to liquidate bank borrowings. This can be effected by straightforward disposal of freeholds or leaseholds, or by sale and leaseback.

Maintenance Planning

Introduction

Property is essentially a long-term investment. Whether held freehold or leasehold its occupation entails a lengthy and ongoing commitment to maintenance, redecoration and obligations whether the latter be to the landlord, to a local authority or others. If held leasehold then despite the sale of the interest, some level of commitment to the COVENANTS contained in the lease may well continue even if only on a contingent basis.

Commitment

Occupiers should develop a philosophy and procedure for ensuring their property assets are properly maintained and that adequate resources are devoted to them. It is all too easy to use a freehold property within the business totally overlooking the need to keep it in good condition. This is less likely to occur with leased property as the landlord may well act as a goad to ensure that the repairing and redecorating covenants are complied with.

Failure to maintain property regularly tends to result in large and unbudgeted expenditure often occurring when it is least expected and least wanted.

Usage

This problem is even more severe when there is high usage of the asset. Whilst this can be regarded as highly beneficial (since the asset is being well used), from the building administration perspective this can cause potentially serious problems. Buildings with high usage are likely to suffer more from damage and deterioration of decoration, whilst the very fact that they are well-used often causes repairs and redecoration to be postponed until 'more convenient times' (or causes considerable disruption and thus poor execution when redecorations are eventually effected).

If routine maintenance is neglected either because of high usage and/or because funds are used elsewhere this can lead to a situation where defects are aggravated and items that could have been dealt with at relative low cost develop into more serious and costly repairs. With leasehold property this problem can culminate in the service by the landlord of a SCHEDULE OF DILAPIDATIONS.

Budgetary control

Resources are almost always limited and, since property tends to have a low profile in the average organisation, it is all too easy for other demands to take priority. This needs to be guarded against and a budget allocated solely for the purposes of keeping buildings in a fair state of repair and redecoration.

There is often a temptation, when under financial pressure, for such budgets to be cut. This should be resisted as almost inevitably these costs will need to be met by the organisation sooner or later. Cutting a current property maintenance budget may have the effect of mortgaging future income. Very often organisations need to expend resources in an emergency well in excess of that which they would have spent on regular maintenance.

Budgets tend to be required on an annual basis which may not be the most cost-effective way of attaining the aims set out above. A longer-term budget with the ability to move the timing of expenditure around may be preferable, as is set out below.

Maintenance plan

1. A property maintenance cycle should be established. This could run for five or more years. All expenditure anticipated in respect of all properties during this period should be costed and plotted on a time of incidence basis.

   Note If there is a PROPERTY REGISTER in use this can provide both a base and a means of recording the agreed process.

2. Regardless of whether buildings are leasehold or freehold, all should be allocated a repair/redecoration programme. Leasehold properties will normally have such a programme set out as one of the lease COVENANTS but a similar programme needs to be developed for freehold properties.

3. Where there is a mixed portfolio (i.e. both freehold and leasehold properties) there may be scope for staging requirements for freehold

MAINTENANCE PLANNING

properties between those for leasehold premises so that the cash effect of both sets of obligations are evened out over the period.

4. If properties need to be developed or extended during the period such costs should be built into the plan.

5. To ensure adequate costing is built into the plan, surveys of the state of the building, plant and equipment need to be conducted and estimates put on the life/investment required (see below). The aim should be to avoid surprises when unexpected costs are incurred due to inadequate maintenance and/or repair.

6. Once a five year (or longer) budget has been completed, commitment should be sought to the whole expenditure on the understanding, subject to cash flow constraints, that items may be able to be brought forward or deferred for, say, six months either side of the expected date if this is more cost-effective or convenient. (For example, if the building industry is slack it may be possible to obtain a keen price for work otherwise not due for some months when the industry might be busier and prices harden against the purchaser.)

Time refining consists of analysing the total commitment and moving expenditure around to suit the cash flow and other preferences of the business. This may even be achieved with lease commitments, with or without the permission of the landlord.

7. It may be preferable to use Day 1 prices and at the time of each subsequent budget agree an inflation factor for items still outstanding. Investigation should only be necessary when estimates vary by (say) 5% of the inflation-adjusted figures.

8. The plan should initially cover 5 years on a rolling basis – year 6 being added as year 1 finishes.

Space planning

It should not be overlooked that approaching property maintenance in this way achieves greater awareness of real costs which can be invaluable when considering future space utilisation and comparing costs of alternative facilities. See LONG-TERM PLANNING

Survey

This may be best achieved by retaining a firm of surveyors and engineers to carry out a full structural survey of the properties and plant. However, those who work with and in the property may feel sufficiently experienced (aided by a limited amount of input, possibly from insurance surveyors, or contractors estimating for other works) to estimate the 'life span' of the various items, thus saving the cost of the survey.

If the organisation is felt to be a potential target for TERRORIST ACTION, security requirements might be built into such a survey.

Current condition checklist

Questions such as the following should be asked with, where applicable, estimates for the cost and the timing of repairs.

Note This checklist is not meant to be exhaustive. It should be regarded as a base on which to customise an individual plan.

ROOF

If pitched, is it waterproof with tiles/other covering sound? How old is the covering? What is its expected life from new?

Are timbers or other supports sound?

Have eaves, guttering and fascia boards been checked for wear?

Are chimneys and vents in good repair or in need of re-pointing?

Are chimney-pot caps in position and sound?

If flat, what is its life and when was it last treated?

Are gutters cleared regularly?

WALLS

Are they sound with good quality material?

Are they damp-protected? Do they need such protection?

Is any rendering sound and in good repair?

Is mortar sound or does it require repointing?

WINDOWS and DOORS

Is the expected life of the frames reasonable or is earlier replacement likely?

Is the glass shatterproof? If not, is it worth implementing this protection?

FOUNDATIONS

Are there any problems with construction indicating required repair?

What is the likelihood of an incidence of subsidence and consequential costs?

MAINTENANCE PLANNING

Are drains and sewers sound? (For relatively low costs, specialist contractors can survey this using mobile underground cameras).

Are there any major trees close to the property?

> *Note* If there are, advice may need to be taken before felling them as removing the mass of roots could severely affect the likelihood of subsidence.

NEIGHBOURHOOD PROBLEMS

Are there any problems experienced by neighbours which could have an effect on the organisation's property.

What is the likelihood of flooding, damage to foundations from trees and so on?

PLANNING REQUIREMENTS

Are there any requirements likely to be imposed which could affect the property a) during the life of the plan and b) subsequently?

> *Note* Local authorities are required to have prepared plans showing all anticipated usages. Although the fact that there is a requirement of alteration in the middle future may not affect the plan itself, it might have an impact on the consideration of the future use/retention of the property.

PLANT AND MACHINERY *

What is the expected life/replacement/reconditioning/repair of hot water system, lifts, central heating, boilers, air conditioning, and all other items?

Has the compressed air/compressor system been investigated? What is its expected life?

Has the gas supply system been checked?

> *Note* Since October 1994 all commercial gas installations have been required to have an emergency cut-off switch.

Kitchen equipment (compliance with Food Safety Act), sports and other facilities provided by the organisation must similarly be checked.

ELECTRICAL INSTALLATION *

What is the expected life/replacement/reconditioning/repair of supply/wiring and sockets?

* Expert assistance may be required. Possibly link with insurance surveys.

Marriages of Interests

Introduction

In the simplest form of occupation – where an organisation occupies a property of which it owns the freehold – there is a single interest in the facility. In most other instances there tend to be at least two interests involved – those of the owner and of the occupier. Thus, in a lease there will be at least two interests – landlord and tenant – but there may, in fact, be many more interests. Often a lessee's immediate landlord holds the lease of the property as an underlease from a superior landlord who may themselves have further superior landlord(s). To each of these parties the lease of the facility may have a value. The potential value may be enhanced by merging two or more of their interests.

Effect

In the simplest cases, a lessee or tenant could offer to buy the freehold interest from their landlord or, alternatively, the landlord could offer to 'buy in' the lease from the lessee. In either event the effect is that a single organisation gains control of the rights of both ownership and occupation. The combined interest can then be sold as a freehold with vacant possession. Since being able to offer the property on this basis should, in most cases, enable a greater value to be obtained than would be possible by aggregating the value of both disposals were they to be sold separately, the marriage of the two interests itself may have a value. In such an instance it may be profitable for either party to approach the other to negotiate a purchase of their interest.

In some cases, occupiers and owners do not realise the potential value of their property rights and, if so, the other party may achieve a deal with enhanced profitability in this way. It is therefore important, if approached with such an offer, that those involved should endeavour to obtain not just a realistic value of their interest but also an indication of the likely potential marriage value since, with such knowledge they may be able to negotiate a better offer. Obviously there is a limit to the asking price since there will still need to be enough left in the deal for the other party to wish to go ahead but without a realistic appreciation of the value of the right too low a figure could be accepted.

Proactive strategy

Realisation of potential property transaction profits can only be achieved if there is

(a) an awareness of

   (i) the value of the property(ies).

   (ii) trends in property values (nationally and locally).

   (iii) opportunities on a local basis.

(b) a willingness to be proactive to conclude a deal.

(c) a readiness to interface with other property occupiers and owners.

Information is essential to become aware of the potential whilst expert advice may be essential to ensure the maximum is achieved.

Neighbour Relationships

Introduction

It has been estimated that of all the problems associated with the occupation of property, problems with neighbours more than equal the aggregate of all others. In turn, of problems with neighbours, it has been estimated that the problem of authorised and illegal parking and the denial of and the creation of difficulties in gaining access is easily the greatest. However, there are several other aspects that should be examined.

Assessing problems

In contemplating the acquisition of a property, means of access to and egress from the property as well as facilities for parking both the organisation's vehicles and those of its employees and visitors should be given due consideration. Experience indicates that valued employees can be lost if they find they are unable to park within a reasonable distance of the workplace or their vehicles are damaged whilst so parked.

Consideration should also be given to any existing problems in this regard possibly by making enquiries of those already in residence as well as of the local police. If premises are being obtained on the basis that the organisation may expand whilst at the site, an assessment of the projected requirements should also be made. Whilst an isolated site may pose problems of its own (e.g. security), at least access and parking difficulties should be fewer.

Employment demand

The close proximity of a competing employer may also mitigate against the choice of a particular property. Conversely, provided the employer's conditions and rates of pay are at least competitive, this could be regarded as advantageous as it may enable the best skills to be drawn from an existing pool of labour. If rates of pay are not competitive (and the organisation is not prepared – or able – to keep them competitive) then moving near a competing employer could lose the more valued employees.

Shared resources

Often where there are a number of similar trading organisations, e.g. a retail shopping centre, office complex, manufacturing industrial estate, there can be advantages in such occupation. Many such entities operate their own security forces, janitorial services, pressure groups, etc. Even though there is a cost involved, since it is shared, the service is likely to be provided for a fraction of the cost of setting up an individual arrangement. Further, the fact that such services are known to be available may make the site somewhat more secure and attractive to prospective occupiers thus enhancing the value of the interest.

Joint action

Where a number of similar facilities are available on lease, they may have a common landlord. If the neighbouring tenants are in touch then it may be possible to ensure that action on common areas of concern is effected quickly and even that by concerted action (for example, to resist too great an upward rent review) advantage can be obtained.

Similar action can be orchestrated in dealing with local authorities over planning or other proposals. The pressure that can be brought to bear by numbers acting in harmony will often result in success quite impossible for a single occupier to achieve.

Trespass

Trespass is a civil wrong and a trespasser is defined as someone who:

(a) enters premises or land (or parts thereof) where he or she has no permission or invitation to be.

(b) remains on premises of land (or parts thereof) after the permission to be so present has expired.

(c) leaves or delivers goods on premises or land without authorisation.

Whilst trespass may be a matter for the individual occupier, an arrangement with neighbours who are working outside 'normal' hours, or simply an arrangement for the exchange of information and ideas for combating the nuisance (particularly from children) may help contain or prevent these incursions (see TRESPASSERS).

Effluent, noise and nuisance

Increasingly, control over the creation of noxious fumes, smells, smoke, etc.

is becoming subject to statutory control. However the legal procedures to prevent this nuisance can take some time to become effective and an on-site relationship may result in greater control and provide a swifter remedy than legal measures.

Similarly noise caused by, for example, building works, can be very disruptive to business, yet legal action could take some weeks to become effective, by which time the works may have been completed. If a relationship has been established it may be possible to reach a compromise whereby (for example) noisy work is only undertaken outside specified hours, or for short bursts at pre-determined intervals, etc.

> Note If informal or good-natured requests fail, it may be necessary to take legal action in which case advice should be sought. Generally the courts may be sympathetic to plaintiffs and, as stated above new controls are being introduced. However the authority in this area is still a very old case – Ryland v Fletcher which dates from 1866. In this case the following rule was laid down: 'a person who for his own purposes brings on his lands ... and keeps there anything likely to do mischief if it escapes, must keep it as his peril and, if he does not do so, is prima facie answerable for all the damage which is the natural consequence of its escape'.

Boundary disputes

As in the question of problems of effluent, noise, etc., an informal approach (particularly if a reciprocal arrangement is possible) may avoid many difficulties. In some cases problems can arise from the fact that the extremities of the building are actually on the boundary line. This can render access to the exterior somewhat difficult and although there is now a legal right to enter neighbouring land to gain such access (the Access to Neighbouring Land Act 1993) subject to application to the court, recourse to legal action may be best avoided if possible. The question of ownership or, and responsibility for fences, party walls, etc. may also need to be determined using expert advice.

Party Wall Act 1997

This act came into effect on 1st April 1997 and extends to the rest of England and Wales the existing arrangements regarding ownership of party walls that exists in London. Since the passing of the London Building Acts those with party walls in the capital have had ownership up to the boundary and statutory rights over the other side of the wall – and this is now the position for the rest of England and Wales.

Those who have party walls will be able to:

- repair, rebuild and increase the land capacity of the wall.
- construct a wall that straddles the boundary and,
- carry out works to the wall from the neighbour's building.

However, the owner must serve notice on the adjoining owner who may object to the works, and must reinstate any damage caused to the property on the other side by such works.

The Act also sets up alternative systems for resolving disputes using either:

- a single 'agreed surveyor' who will act as an arbitrator, or,
- the triple surveyor procedure whereby each party appoints a surveyor who then appoint a third surveyor.

Summary

None of the advantages set out above are guaranteed, but equally none are capable of achievement unless there is a reasonable relationship between neighbours. This may take time and resources, but may result in long term savings. Although increasingly there are legal protections, using these may be expensive and will almost certainly damage what is usually a long-term relationship.

Notices

Introduction

Limited liability companies are required to have a 'registered office'. The purpose of this is so that those dealing with the company know the location of an office to which can be sent official notices on a range of matters. The receipt of and generation of action on such notices is a subject which needs to be granted considerable attention as often such notices require action within a set time and failure to act may result in liabilities and/or penalties being borne by the company. Organisations other than companies should similarly nominate an 'administrative office' to which such correspondence should be sent. Such an office should be the location for the executive charged with the responsibility for responding to notices served in connection with the business, perhaps the company secretary or in-house lawyer. Experience indicates that this important facet of property occupation is often overlooked.

Location

When agreeing a lease or licence the address of the registered or administrative office should be stated in the documentation as the place to which all notices should be sent. Where an organisation occupies only one location, this may not cause too much of a problem. However, when additional sites are acquired, particularly where these are not staffed by administrative employees, or those who will realise the importance of notices lodged there, the address of the administrative office should be stated in the leases or licences governing such occupation. Landlords usually prefer to insert a provision that notice will be served at the location demised by the lease, etc., and if they are unwilling to agree to change this, then the address of the administrative office should be inserted as the place where an additional copy of the notice must be served. In this way, at least the chance of the notice being drawn to the attention of someone who can realise its significance is doubled. It is also good practice to advise those in satellite locations that all notices must immediately be passed to [a nominated person].

> *Note* The term 'administrative office' has been used deliberately to draw attention to the location where notices must be sent. If the words 'registered office' are used then notices can be sent there. This may not be convenient where the registered office is not the location of the property administrator.

Change of administrative office

If the administrative office itself changes then the landlords of all leases and licences specifying the address should be notified by recorded delivery with a covering letter in duplicate. They should be asked to sign and return the copy covering letter confirming they have altered their records accordingly. If a notice is subsequently served on the incorrect address at least the receipt is available as evidence of the change and its acceptance. Companies House must also be informed under Section 287 of the Companies Act 1985 which sets out all the detailed requirements for the registered office.

Procedure

Most leases and licences specify in exact terms how notices are to be served, and on receipt of a notice such terminology should be referred to a) to check the notice is properly served and b) as a reminder of the action to be taken and within what time limit.

The following should be checked:

(a) The address on which notice is to be served and that it has been served on that address.

(b) Time limit within which it must be served and that it has been served in accordance with such time limits.

(c) That the notice is issued by the person authorised to do so by the lease terms.

(d) That the wording is in accordance with that set out in the lease (if any).

(e) That any specific method of serving is as stipulated.

If any aspect of notice is not in accordance with one or more of these requirements, it may be possible to reject the notice and for it to be returned to the sender with the advice that it is considered that the notice is invalid. Specific advice should be taken in such an instance as minor irregularities may not be sufficient to render the notice invalid.

NOTICES

Timing

If, however, the notice is out of time, it may be possible to reject it which would mean that either the action the notice was intended to start (e.g. a rent review) cannot commence, or that the action must be delayed until the serving of a fresh notice. Whilst late serving will not normally invalidate the notice, should the terminology state that 'time is of the essence' then it may be that the action is lost. It may be advisable to take legal advice.

Late serving of a notice to terminate a lease has the effect of extending the lease term until the expiry of six months from the date of the notice.

Action

Very often the notice will require the recipient to acknowledge receipt with a duplicate notice enclosed for return to effect this. If the lease requires the lessee to acknowledge receipt this should be complied with. Otherwise the requirements of the lease as to the lessee's action should be checked and carried out to the letter.

In replying to the notice of a rent review, lessees are sometimes required not just to object to any figure proposed by the landlord but also to state their valuation of the rent at the review date. If so a figure should be inserted. The assessment of this figure needs some thought.

(a) With a lease that has an upwards-only rent review clause, the current rent should be inserted (since the rent cannot be less than that figure in any case).

(b) With a lease without upwards only protection for the landlord, the tenant should check the local area to gain a reasoned assessment of the levels of rent and insert a figure around (say) 80% of that figure in case rents decline between the date of the notice and of the review itself. In writing to state this figure the words 'Without prejudice' should be inserted on the letter or counter-notice. This means that the figure cannot be produced in court and is a protection in case, during negotiations, the lessee realises their assessment is too high.

> *Note* *It should not be overlooked that the fact that the end of the term of years granted by a lease has occurred does not of itself bring the lease to an end for either party. The action required of the landlord is detailed above, but should the lessee wish to terminate occupation at the end of the lease then they too must serve notices. In this situation advice should be taken.*

Action for the lessee to terminate the lease should be considered where the lessee feels that as a result of an upwards-only rent review clause, the existing rent is higher than might be the case with a new lease. In such circumstances it is possible that the landlord will not bring the lease to an end but merely allow it to continue – at the existing rent.

Obtaining Value

Introduction

The main purpose of a business acquiring property, or acquiring the right to occupy property, should be to facilitate the aims and purposes of the business itself, i.e. to enable the production of widgets, the sale or storage of goods or the provision of services, etc. However, since investing in property is a long-term undertaking, it should not be overlooked that property assets themselves may command a value which can be used in the business. Whilst not advocating that businesses should speculate in property – unless of course that is their business – proper maintenance and control of a property portfolio should require that occupiers constantly reassess the underlying value of the property in case such value can be released.

Sale and leaseback

The simplest method of releasing value from property is selling the freehold interest to a property investor whilst immediately taking a lease of the same property from the new owner. Thus the occupation of the property does not change. The former freehold owner now has a lease of the premises and is of course responsible for the various responsibilities and covenants set out in the lease. Since the former owner will have a certain amount of control over the negotiations it may be possible to formulate a lease which contains quite advantageous terms although the more advantageous these become the less may be the capital sum obtained from the sale of the freehold. Thus it may be necessary to balance short-term cash needs against the ongoing lease commitments.

Internal rents for use of freehold

Organisations that own and trade from freeholds need to appreciate that their current profitability may be augmented as a result of an advantageous property deal in the past. For example, if a freehold was purchased, say, 25 years previously, the amount paid for the acquisition may be very small compared to the amount that would have to be paid for the same property even in the current depressed property market. Where trading is being conducted from a number of units of mixed ownership, comparability between units cannot be properly achieved. The imposition of regular rent reviews (reflecting the level of rents being charged currently in the neighbourhood) may mean that leased units are fully charged whereas those in freeholds are not so exposed.

To ensure each unit bears an appropriate level of expenditure, regular revaluations of the freehold properties could be carried out (e.g. every five years to equate to the normal frequency of lease rent reviews) and an internal rent, calculated by reference to that valuation could be charged against the income (or levied as an expense item) of the unit. Not only does this create comparability between units, it also exposes the profitability of the unit to a near true cost of their occupation of the property.

Whilst no additional value has been created (although operating units will have been charged a 'rent' which can be credited to a property division or similar account), the exercise should help encourage objective consideration of the value of the business at the location.

Charging property

Since, over a long period, freehold values generally tend to appreciate, many organisations that own freeholds regard them as a form of investment or even saving for the future. Whilst long-term value appreciation cannot be denied what needs to be assessed is the rate of return compared to the rate of return that could be achieved were the value commanded by the freehold(s) invested in the business itself or other investments.

However, outright sale is not the only method by which cash can be raised for use in the business. Freehold property is usually highly acceptable security for a loan. By creating a legal charge over property, banks and others may be prepared to advance cash or to increase an overdraft. Companies which charge such assets must enter details of the charge(s) in a Register kept for this purpose which must be made available for inspection by all-comers for at least two hours each business day. The charge must be registered with the Registrar of Companies under Section S.395 of the Companies Act 1985 within 21 days of its creation.

Becoming a landlord

The realisation of the value of freeholds and the imposition of internal rents may force reconsideration of the use of property within the business. With buoyant demand in the property market it may be even more profitable to cease the business carried on at certain premises (either totally or transferring it to other sites) and to lease out the property. This is a policy which can also be considered (for both freeholds and, provided the lease permits, for leaseholds) if property assets are not required for a short term within the business – a situation which should be disclosed by LONG-TERM PLANNING. Subletting for shorter or longer periods may create property management demands on the organisation but it should ensure that value is obtained from property assets during the time that they are surplus to requirements.

Relocation

A number of organisations, particularly within the financial services industry and located in London, realised when faced by the capital's rising occupation costs during the 1980s that, if they relocated their operation out of London, they could release funds tied up in property. A number of large and valuable premises in prestigious locations were sold and replaced by less costly alternatives in other parts of the country such as Bristol, Cardiff, Peterborough, etc. This did not always entail losing a presence in the old site – sometimes a much smaller facility was retained to ensure access to the facilities in the old location thought to be particularly valuable. In fact, with modern communication systems and increasingly fast methods of transportation, often the 'perceived need' to use the former facilities was found to have been overrated.

Marriages of interests

The principle of achieving greater value for a property asset by merging two or more interests is set out in MARRIAGES OF INTERESTS. In considering releasing value from property assets this aspect of property trading should not be overlooked either on a sole basis or in partnership with a landlord or tenant.

Renegotiating a term

Institutional property owners regard their properties virtually as commodities. Like all commodities the value of the 'stock' fluctuates and the value of a lease (even with a lessee with a good 'covenant' (i.e. a reputation for financial dependability and prompt payments, etc.) will diminish as it nears the end of its term. In such circumstances it can happen that the institution will approach the lessee to try to negotiate a new term before the old one has ended. Agreement to this arrangement by the lessee closes off the opportunity of the lessee negotiating the rent (for the first segment of a new lease) from a position of greater strength than it would have at a rent review. Accordingly the lessee should be able to ask for some value (e.g. a substantial rent-free period) as a quid pro quo.

Summary

Investing in property entails a long term commitment. Conversely technological and demand changes are occurring at an ever faster rate which makes planning for the long term increasingly difficult to such an extent that outlines of intent may be all that can be given. In such circumstances it is essential that a very proactive attitude is taken to the value locked into property assets.

Occupier's Liability

Introduction

Under pain of criminal liability and sanctions, organisations occupying property have obligations to those that work there to provide a safe place and means of work (see HEALTH AND SAFETY). In addition, extensive duties of care are owed by occupiers to visitors, those engaged on building and similar work at the premises, and also to those whom the organisation wishes to prevent being there such as trespassers, etc. There have been two Acts of Parliament dealing with the duties owed to persons on the premises, the Occupiers Liability Acts of 1957 and 1984.

The 1957 Act

An occupier of premises (who is defined as someone who has comprehensive control over part but not necessarily all of the premises) is required under this Act to 'take such care as in all the circumstances of the case is reasonable to see that the visitor will be reasonably safe in using the premises for the purposes for which he is invited or permitted by the occupier to be there'.

If the occupier is negligent in providing safe premises then the person injured has a right of civil action provided he was a visitor or was invited on to the premises. Under this Act no protection was granted to trespassers or to those, for example, exercising a right of way through the premises.

If there are areas in the premises which are dangerous then proper signs warning of the danger, guard rails, etc. should be utilised to protect those who could be at risk.

An occupier may be able to escape liability to those suffering as a result of accidents at the premises if they are capable of being regarded as having skills which should prepare them to avoid such dangers. For example, appointing a reputable firm of builders who it can be assumed would be aware of the dangers inherent in building works, might absolve from liability an occupier should one or more of the builders suffer an accident whilst engaged on such works. Conversely, if the work required was very specialised then the occupier would have to show that he deliberately employed those known to have such specialist skills in order to escape liability.

Duty to children

The Act recognised that occupiers had special duties in relation to children who would not always recognise danger, or even take note of signs warning of danger. The Act therefore stated that 'an occupier must be prepared for children to be less careful than adults'. Objects (ladders, waste material, brightly coloured drums, etc.) could prove to be attractive to children and act as a lure to them. If so such objects could be regarded as a trap and thus the occupier could become liable for injury to a child even though the child was trespassing.

However, if it can be shown that the trespasser, even if a child, had 'willingly accepted the risks' then there may be no duty of care. Such a defence could be mounted if, for example it could be shown that the child had been warned of the danger and told not to play there, etc. Even in such a case, the occupier would have to show that they had taken all reasonable steps to deter the trespass.

In the case of *Adams v Southern Electricity Board* a boy often climbed and played around the pole-mounted transformer installation near his home. Although the Board had erected protective devices to try to deter such actions these became inoperative and the boy was electrocuted. The Court of Appeal held that even though it could be said that the boy had become immune to the danger, the Board was in breach of its common law obligation to take reasonable care for the boy's safety.

In the case of *Margereson & Hancock v J W Roberts Ltd*, the company was held to be liable to the widow of a man who had contracted a disease as a result of him playing, when a child, in the asbestos-ridden dust of their loading bay even though he had had no right to be.

Custom and practice

Under the 1957 Act no duty of care was owed to those not entitled to be on the premises, unless any injury or damage suffered by such persons was caused as a result of some deliberate act on the part of the occupier, or action was taken with a disregard for such a person's safety, e.g. leaving dangerous dogs roaming the premises freely, or deliberately setting traps. However, following the 1957 Act, case law developed which began to hold that occupiers did have a duty of care to those without rights of access, e.g. those who trespassed. For example, in the *British Railways Board v Herrington* appeal in 1972, the principle established was that if the occupier knew before the accident that there was a probability of trespassers, then a failure to give consideration for their safety could be culpable.

The 1984 Act

This Act brought into the legal framework the attitude demonstrated by comments such as those made in the Railways Board case of 1972 and placed a duty of care on an occupier in respect of trespassers as well as those legally present. If a trespasser suffers an accident whilst on the premises then the occupier can be held liable for the accident if he:

(a) was aware of the danger.

(b) believes that it is possible that a trespasser could enter the vicinity of the danger.

(c) could reasonably be expected to have offered or afforded some protection from the danger.

The standard of care owed to a trespasser is lower than that due to a legitimate visitor and is 'to take such care as is reasonable in all the circumstances of the case to see that he does not suffer injury on the premises by reason of the danger concerned'.

Adequate security measures are essential not just against those who wish to damage and steal but also against those who wish to play.

Liability to contractors and employees

Under HEALTH AND SAFETY legislation, an employer owes a duty of care to employees working on business premises (and to contractors brought on to those premises) and must prepare a health and safety policy. In addition, for BUILDING WORKS on the premises, a safety plan must be prepared. Where contractors enter working premises they should be required to comply with both the health and safety policy and any safety plan.

Case studies

In the case of *R v Gateway Foodmarkets* the company was held to be liable for the death of an employee who had been shown (by contractors) how to override an electrical fault to operate a lift. The company was unaware that this kind of manual override was common practice.

In another case (*R v Rhone Poulenc Rorer Ltd*), an employer had written procedures but were held liable when a sub-contractor (in defiance of instructions to the contrary) climbed on to a roof and fell to his death through a rooflight. The court held that the company should have provided a guard rail or some other physical precaution to prevent injury.

Options to break

Introduction

Generally, leases of premises run for a fixed term of years with the original terms broken only by the need for regular reviews of the rent. However in some instances it may be in the interests of the lessee or the landlord, or even both, to be able to bring the relationship to an end before the natural term of the agreement by means of an option which has the effect of breaking the term and bringing the lease to a premature end.

Grant

Except in very special circumstances where both parties agree to vary the term of a lease by mutually agreeing to bring it to a premature end – perhaps because there is the possibility of both acquiring value from a third party by means of a MARRIAGE OF INTERESTS – a lease normally runs until its termination date. However, for a variety of reasons, either or both parties may want to insert in the lease (when agreeing terms) an option to determine the lease at a time earlier than its stated expiry date.

WARNING As far as the lessee is concerned, care should be taken to try to time the operative date of any option to follow (rather than precede) a rent review since in this way the occupancy cost for the period until the next review will be known before the option must be exercised.

Rationale

The reasons for requesting a break could be:

(a) because the lessee (for example, being in a new business) is unsure of the capacity of the business to exist for the full term of the lease, or exist at a level where the outgoings are sustainable.

(b) because the Landlord may want to redevelop the site (for example most of the leases issued by London Transport contain a six-month break clause at the landlord's discretion in case they need to acquire occupation for the purpose of redevelopment).

(c) because both parties want to try the relationship which if it works in the short term can be allowed to continue but, if it does not, can be terminated.

In each of these examples, the option clauses can be phrased in different ways – i.e. they can be exercised at the volition of the lessee, the landlord or both.

Implementation

(a) Lessee's option

The lease will set out the procedure for generating the break clause and it is essential that, not only is the exact procedure followed, but also that the remainder of the COVENANTS are complied with. The exercise of a lessee's option may not be welcomed by the landlord (since it means an empty property to be marketed and a potential loss of rent whilst the property is vacant). For this reason, landlords do sometimes resist the exercise of an option by suggesting that, since the lessee has not complied with other covenants required of them under the lease, they are thus in breach and cannot exercise the option validly. Thus it is important to ensure that there is total compliance with the covenants – rent paid on time, repair and redecoration timetable up to date and so on.

> *Note* *Sufficient time should be left to allow for any queries to be resolved prior to crucial dates. For example, if the lease does not state on whom a notice exercising an option is to be served clarification should be sought well in advance, with any letter requesting clarification being sent recorded delivery and requesting a reply within (say) 14 days. In the event of any ambiguity advice should be sought.*

(b) Landlord's option

Again, the means and method by which the landlord can exercise the option to break should be laid down in the lease and the exact procedure must be observed.

Termination

The exact way in which termination is effected following the exercise of an option should be laid down in the lease. If the landlord accepts a lessee's option, it is prudent to expect service of a SCHEDULE OF DILAPIDATIONS and prompt execution will be needed to ensure the work is completed prior to vacation. Where the landlord exercises the option, compliance with the requirements will be expected of the lessee although again a SCHEDULE OF DILAPIDATIONS may be served.

Awareness

The fact that there is an option clause should be noted in the property PRECIS and suitable reminders inserted so that if notice is required preparations can take place in sufficient time to allow all necessary checks to be made.

Payments

> **Introduction**
>
> All payments in respect of property occupation should be checked for accuracy and timing. Although this may be stating the obvious, there is a fairly widespread belief that since 'property payments' are levied by external sources they 'must be right'. This is not always the case. Thus no assumptions as to accuracy should be made and back-up authority for every item should be sought. Suggestions for verifying accounts in a variety of situations are set out below.

Rent

The amount demanded should be checked against the lease PRECIS and/or property calendar. If interest is demanded on late payment, check the lease or precis to ensure that it allows the principle of such charge and that the interest rate charged is in accordance with that allowed by the lease. Note that many leases state that rent is payable whether demanded or not, and thus non-receipt of a demand is not a valid reason for non-payment. This would mean that late payment could attract an interest charge even though no demand had been received. It may be prudent to ensure that rent cheques are drawn in advance of the due date.

In the first and last quarter of a lease term there may be a need to apportion the rent in respect of a split quarter. The basis of the calculation may need clarifying. Rent claimed on the basis of a proportion of a quarter may give rise to a higher amount due than rent claimed on the basis of annual rent on a daily basis.

VAT on rent

At the option of landlords VAT can be added to rent. Since landlords are required to advise lessees before they take such action, if a rent demand bears a VAT charge, check that the landlord has advised that VAT will be payable. Also check that a proper VAT invoice is received since not all rent demands are VAT invoices.

Rent increase

If the rent has been increased, check that the date from which the new rent is payable is as agreed in the lease and/or RENT REVIEW MEMORANDUM. If interest is payable on late settlement of a reviewed rent, check that the rate and amount charged are correct.

> *Note* It is not always the case that an increase agreed after the relevant review date is backdated to that date – it depends on the wording of the lease. If the landlord was late starting the review process then some (older) leases state that the new rent becomes effective only from the date 'when agreed'. Further it may be that any interest payable in respect of 'late agreement' can only be levied from that date. To offset the incentive for the lessee to drag out the review procedure – thereby delaying the impact of any increased rent – the Landlord should ensure that every effort is made to attain a speedy resolution.

Rent-free period.

If work is required to the premises before occupation (or even during it), the landlord may be prepared to allow a period of occupation 'rent free' whilst such work is completed. This should always be evidenced in writing and this can serve as the document of record to check that the amount of credit that has been agreed is allowed in the calculation.

Insurance

Check cover against the lease requirements, the sum insured for adequacy, as well as the premium demanded against market rate. See INSURANCE re challenging premiums re-charged.

> **WARNING** If the landlord is allowed to recharge insurance premiums the charge is known as 'insurance rent'. To recover such an item, landlords can distrain for payment. Distraining means that bailiffs can be sent in to seize property to the value of the amount disputed. This can be done without the landlord needing to obtain a court order.

Utility charges (shared supply)

Check the appropriateness of the apportionment and request a copy of the original invoice. If metered, check charge against meter records. Meters should be read by an employee at the same time as the supply company inspection.

Utility charges (individual supply)

Check against meter readings and review against prior year for usage comparison.

Service charge

Check that the services being charged for are as agreed in the lease; that the proportion being charged is correct and is in accordance with the lease, and with the original statement showing how total costs were to be calculated. If the lease states that any such statement is to be supported by an auditor's or other certificate, ensure receipt of such certificate and check amount required against that. Try to ensure that amounts regarding any under-or non-payment on behalf of any lessee(s) are not to be recouped from other lessees.

Repairs and/or redecoration

Check the principle and the responsibility against the lease requirements and that what is required is in accordance with a previous estimate. Usually the obligation is on the lessee to arrange for repairs, etc. and thus an approved estimate should already be available. Checks should be conducted to ensure that the work has been carried out in accordance with the specification and estimate and that it is of acceptable standard. The full amount of the contract should not be paid until the end of any defects liability period. Thus there needs to be a retention amount (usually 5% or 10%) deducted from each payment (see BUILDING WORKS).

Dilapidations

Check that there is a right of service of such a schedule under the lease terms, and that it is in accordance with the schedule of work agreed which should itself have been the subject of discussion/agreement between surveyors appointed by the two parties.

Rates

Check that the demand is in accordance with any RATING or rerating proposal. It may also be necessary to consider whether to appeal against the assessment.

Telephone

If abuse is suspected, call-recording machinery can be installed which will provide a print-out of every number called – even showing the extension used. Internal extensions can be barred from access to the outside line system although they can accept incoming calls.

> **WARNING** If call-recording machinery is installed someone must check the printout regularly in order to set up investigations of abuse. If there is no investigation when there is abuse not only will the organisation be paying for private calls, it will also be bearing the cost of the non-productive equipment. It must be noted that there are strict laws on taping outside calls. Callers must be told that they are being recorded.

Occupational charges

Invoices for regular maintenance contracts (e.g. roof and gutter clearing, window cleaning, gardening, etc.) should be checked for accuracy and agreement with the estimate. At the times of such work, someone should be required to inspect the work and its completion and make a note of this so that the invoice can be authorised.

Planning Applications

Introduction

Although owners of freehold property have far wider scope for using their property in a variety of ways than do occupiers of leased property who will normally need to obtain the consent of the landlord to any alterations, etc. (including use), both types of property are subject to local planning requirements and alterations (particularly to the use and/or exterior of the premises) will require consent. Some properties are listed and require additional consents.

Scope

The scope of planning authorities is wide and has grown rapidly over a relatively short time. The main principle to remember is that alterations to the use and fabric of a property will almost certainly require planning approval. Unfortunately the simplicity of this over-riding consideration can be contrasted with the considerable complexity of the mass of planning laws and regulations. Detailed guidance to planning requirements is outside the scope of this book. Nevertheless, the following checklist (the first part of which is drawn from the Department of the Environment's own advice) can be a useful starting point. With anything other than the most routine alteration, expert advice should be obtained. It should be noted that proceeding without consent could incur substantial costs including the removal and/or demolition of any structure or works.

Procedure

1. Visit the planning officer. Describe what the organisation wishes to do, showing the outline plans.

2. Ask for assessment of whether there seems a reasonable chance of obtaining permission on the current basis.

3. If not, enquire whether there is any way of modifying the plans which would help to obtain consent.

Note *The point about gaining this input at this stage is that sometimes quite minor alterations can ensure approval, whilst if major alterations are necessary, or the entire proposal is unacceptable, knowledge before too much time and resources are wasted is essential.*

4. Ask advice on various matters such as roads, footpaths, power cables, watercourses, sewers, telephone lines or toxicity.

   Note *Under developing ENVIRONMENT PROTECTION legislation, local authorities are gaining wide powers to prevent land contamination and to require the cleansing of such land.*

5. Discuss problems re noise, traffic, etc.

6. Discuss the possibility of the authority applying any conditions and then consider the effect of these on the proposals.

7. Query whether publicity of intentions is essential.

8. Ask for the timetable of planning committee meetings.

   Note *Since these meetings tend to be held every 4-6 weeks, timing, particularly with a complex building operation, could be vital.*

9. Check the costs involved. Authorities are allowed to charge for planning considerations up to a maximum of £5500, or even more if the subject is related to the use of land for the disposal of waste, etc.

10. Leave plenty of time for the whole process. Informal discussions such as the above can be invaluable but themselves can take time particularly if plans and specifications have to be altered and then put through the meeting process.

Listed buildings

The whole process of planning, renovations and repairing is further complicated if the building is listed. It is essential that experienced staff handle such matters and advice is taken at a very early stage particularly since any works already carried out may be required to be removed and reinstatement made.

Other planning applications

Local authorities have powers to grant planning applications and also (and subsequently) to revoke or alter the term of such permission. In addition, any person who develops land or erects, alters or extends a building without permission where permission is required, can be served an enforcement notice by the planning authority requiring compliance with the terms of that order. Such terms could even include demolition of the works. Failure to comply with such an order is a criminal offence. In addition, Planning Contravention notices can be served which requires the addressee to provide information. Failure to comply (including failure to provide the information within 21 days) is also a criminal offence.

The Department of the Environment's booklets *Planning Permission – a guide for small businesses* and *Planning appeals,* are valuable introductory guides.

Précis

Introduction

Modern leases and conveyances tend to be complicated documents where both the size of the documents as well as the language used are anything but user-friendly. Both these factors also make it difficult to find the required reference with any ease, although a welcome development is the inclusion of a contents list in some leases. For the busy property administrator time may be so much of the essence that instant guidance to the salient features of both documents (and any others that bear on the use and exploitation of the property) is essential. This can be achieved by using a précis which can not only provide an instant guide but also, if a standard format is used for all leases, provide a guide within a guide since the same information will always be found in the same place. In addition a comprehensive system of a précis for each property provides a data bank from which can be drawn the skeletal information essential to produce a PROPERTY REGISTER.

Freehold précis

Organisation name   Freehold précis sheet
Address of property   Internal ref. number
Date of purchase   Price
Finance details
Land Charge Certificate data
Conveyance data
Ground rent (if applicable, specify review terms, etc)

Third party rights over the premises (if any) (i.e. those of a mortgagor, in which case a synopsis of the terms of the mortgage, repayments, terms, etc., should be incorporated)

Details of any shared rights of access over land/premises (i.e. use of land retained to a neighbour, shared facilities, etc., including details of anyone holding and/or administering such rights)

Any charge registered on the property (in which case it may be convenient to attach a copy of the documentation lodged with the Registrar of Companies and form 395).

Details of all consents, wayleaves, advertising sign agreements, etc., with names and addresses of the parties involved, and synopsis of the terms.

Details of all obligations required as a term of the sale/acquisition, with a dated entry made once the work has been completed, the cost involved and any guarantee given in respect of the work

Use within business (specify)

Revaluation data

Internal market rent (if any) (see OBTAINING VALUE)

Future requirements (see LONG-TERM PLANNING)

Special features or restrictions

Areas (Zoning and Zone A equivalents for retail premises, net internal for offices, gross internal for industrial premises)

Leasehold précis

Organisation name	Leasehold précis sheet
Address of property	Internal ref. number
Landlord	
Agent	
Guarantor	
Date of acquisition Price	
Unit data	
Rent £ p.a. payable	to
Days grace?	VAT payable?
Interest on late payment?	
Lease terms: Date of lease	
Date of commencement	and termination
User (and any variation)	
Assignment (details and restrictions)	
Subletting (details and restrictions)	
Reviews dates	
Procedure on review	
Interest on late agreement YES/NO	

PRÉCIS

If YES, from what and at what rate

Covenants   Repair (due dates)
                Redecoration (due dates)
                Insurance (basis of covers, and responsibility)
                Service charge (details and basis)
                Other (specify)
                Other

Does Privity of Contract apply?

Option to break (if any)

Procedure re option

Floor area (retail)   Zone A   sq ft.
                         Zone B   sq ft.
                         Zone C   sq ft.

Storage

Other

Net internal area (offices)

Gross area (industrial premises)

Parking arrangements

Parking costs

Special features or restrictions

Comments

Subletting

It should not be overlooked that in both types of occupation there may be sublets and thus a subletting précis (i.e. a slightly amended leasehold précis) completed with details of the sublet(s), could accompany the main précis sheet. It may be helpful to use coloured sheets for the subletting précis to differentiate them from those of units occupied for the organisation's business purposes.

Privity of Contract

Introduction

Until 1 January 1996 when the Landlord and Tenant (Covenants) Act 1995 came into force, leases of commercial property were subject to the Privity of Contract rule. The 1995 Act abolished the Privity rule for all leases entered into on or after that day although landlords will have the right to request lessees to provide GUARANTEES which to some extent may have the same effect as the old privity rule.

Definition

Under the Privity of Contract rule, despite subsequent assignment of the interest in a lease, the original lessee retains the ultimate responsibility to the landlord for the payment of outgoings set out in the lease. The effect of this is that if the original lessee (X) assigns his interest to a new lessee (A) the landlord gains privity of estate against the new lessee. However, if the new lessee defaults then the landlord can recharge X with the amount of the default. Although initially X may be able to protect his position by checking the financial probity of A, taking up references, etc., this is no long-term guarantee. He could ask for a deposit of one years rent in case of default although this may prove impossible to attain.

Such protections (limited as they are) are of little use to X if A assigns his interest to B and B then assigns the interest to C as it is unlikely, even if X knows of the further assignments, that he can have any control whatever over them. The situation is even worse for individuals that may have guaranteed the original lease to X, if X itself has ceased trading. In that case, the landlord may well have a right of action against the guarantors.

The new law

The Act's main provisions are listed below.

(a) If the lease allows unrestricted assignment, then an assigning tenant is released from the lease covenants.

(b) If (as is more normally the case) the lease allows for assignment but subject to landlord's consent, then the landlord can impose conditions, i.e. that the assigning tenant agrees to guarantee the performance of the incoming tenant to the lease covenant obligations. This is known as an Authorised Guarantee Agreement (AGA) which is limited to the immediate assignee only. In such circumstances, of course, the assigning tenant would still be liable in the event of default, but only the default of the assignee with whom he contracted. (In the example given above, X would be liable if A defaulted, but not B or C.) If the new lessee assigns in turn then the landlord can ask for an AGA to be entered into, thus in the example above A would be asked to enter into an AGA in respect of B and would be liable if B (only) defaulted.

The conditions under which an assignment can be granted can be agreed by the parties at the time the lease is negotiated.

(c) As far as rent and service charges are concerned, the guarantee of the original tenant is restricted to those amounts demanded by the landlord within six months of them falling due.

Note   This proviso applies to all leases whether they were in operation as at 1 January 1996 or prior to that date.

(d) If a tenant is required to pay arrears they can require the landlord to grant them a lease of the premises (thus giving them the right of occupation of the premises).

Effect

An immediate effect may be that landlords may refuse to allow rights of assignment in new leases, although the counter to that is that lessees would presumably then ask for much shorter leases and/or the inclusion of a break option, in order to retain flexibility. It is possible that the valuation of leases could be affected depending on whether or not the Privity of Contract rule applied.

Property Register

Introduction

For an administrator with a property portfolio of – say, ten or more units – some kind of simplified analysis or register of the salient features of the various properties can be very valuable to provide instantly accessible information. However, taking this one stage further, such a register can be used for forecasting as well as providing historical information. If using a grid format projected for say 15 – 20 years, not only is salient written information available in one place incorporating warning of future expenditure, but also an instant visual picture can be created of the portfolio as it will appear at any one time in the period covered. In addition, a register can provide a guide at times of planning and budgeting.

Format

The register can be produced either as hard copy or in a computerised format. The advantage of the computerised record is that it can be updated easily although there may be an advantage in retaining old information (albeit 'crossed through' in some way) in order to show history. This will be particularly valuable in tracing increases in rent, previous tenants, etc. Once the grid has been determined then the information can be inserted preferably using the PRECIS sheets already prepared as these should disclose the required information more easily than will reference to the original documents – conveyance, lease, TENANCY AGREEMENT, etc.

Guide to the register

Inspection of the entries included for example purposes will disclose:

(a) a cross-section of the types of occupation – freehold, freehold with sublet, leasehold, leasehold with sublet, etc.

(b) the salient features of the address together with contact names and telephone numbers. Such contact could include:

(i) for owned and occupied premises, the name of the senior person present.

(ii) for owned and sublet premises, the name of the tenant.

(iii) for leased and occupied premises, the name of the landlord or agent.

(iv) for leased and sub leased premises, the name of the landlord or agent and the tenant.

(c) where the property is leasehold:

(i) the term of the lease and the expiry dates.

(ii) the rent with previous rents crossed through (but left legible).

(iii) details of the incidence of rent reviews.

(iv) the intervals after which redecorations are required on both an internal and external basis (or as applicable).

(v) notes regarding the liability for insuring and any right to sublet (or bar against this).

(vi) the size of the property (and an indication of whether this has been agreed with the landlord – see RENT REVIEW).

(viii) the user and any restrictions (in some cases this may be so complicated that reference may need to be made to the précis).

ix) a calendar in which is inserted the incidence of all reviews, redecoration times, options to break and termination dates.

(d) where the property is sublet:

(i) the term and expiry date.

(ii) rents charged and updated.

(iii) details of any rent reviews.

(iv) the intervals after which redecorations are required on both an internal and external basis (or as applicable).

(v) notes regarding the liability for insurance if allowed to the lessee.

vi) the size of the property (and an indication of whether this has been agreed with the lessee – see RENT REVIEW).

vii) any restrictions on the user.

e) where the property is freehold and is used in the business: similar information to that shown above but in addition the valuations of the internal rents charged so that it is immediately apparent what return is being obtained for the use of the property.

Freehold Portfolio

Property	Price/date purchased	Location of deeds	Contact	Redecoration int	Redecoration ext	Res.	Sq FT	Use	96	97	98	99	00	01	02	03	04	05	06	07
111 Haymarket, Bristol	£265,000 9/90	Bank	(name)	3 yrly	3 yrly	None	B: 600 G: 1000 1st: 800 2nd: 800	Office Store	IE			IE		IE				IE		
											V		V		V		V			V	
																			E		E
22 West Street, Norwich	£70,000 2/84	Bank	(name)	5 yrly	5 yrly	None	B: 750 1st: 600 2nd: 600 Garage	Shop Store	I E				V	I E					V	I E

Notes: 1. Purchase details are recorded. If there were any restrictive covenants these could be inserted under 'RES'. 2. The requirement to redecorate is purely self-imposed. 3. The abbreviations used in this chart are: I = internal redecoration, E = External redecoration, V = valuations.

Freehold Portfolio with Sublet

Property	Price/date purchased	Location of deeds	Contact	Redecoration int	Redecoration ext	Res.	Sq FT	Use	96	97	98	99	00	01	02	03	04	05	06	07
22 West Street, Norwich	£70,000 2/84	Bank	(name)	5 yrly	5 yrly	None	G: 750 1st: 600 2nd: 600 Garage	Shop Store	I E				V	I E					V	I E
	Sublets 1) Grd, 1st + 2nd floors	3/96-3/06 £5,000 R: 3/01	(name of tenant)	3 yrly + last	3 yrly + last			Shop				I E		R	I E			I E		
	2) Garage	Yearly £1,040	(name of tenant)	yearly	yearly			Garage											T	

Notes: 1. The sublet details could follow the layout in the leasehold portfolio or a more simplified layout as here. 2. There is little point in inserting the requirement for the tenant of the garage to redecorate annually in the calendar. 3. The abbreviations used in this chart are: I = internal redecoration, E = external redecoration, R = rent review, T = termination of lease, V = valuations. Valuations may be required on a three or five year cycle.

Lease Portfolio

Property From/To	Term	Rent	Reviews	Redecoration int	Redecoration ext	Ins	Sq FT	User	97	98	99	00	01	02	03	04	05	06	07
17 Highgate Lane, London Contact: (Name)	20 yrs 6/85–6/05	~~£10,000~~ ~~£16,500~~ £17,000	~~90~~ ~~95~~ 00	5 yrly	7 yrly + Last	Company	1250	Class		E	I R						I E T		
24 Broadway, Manchester Contact: (Name)	20 yrs 9/87–9/07	~~£11,500~~ £17,000	~~92~~ 97 02 Option 97	5 yrly	3 yrly	Landlord + Recharge	1000	See Précis	I R O	E			I E R				E		T
62 Haymarket, Bristol Contact: (Name)	15 yrs 3/90–3/05	~~£12,500~~ ~~£17,800~~ £17,800	~~93~~ ~~96~~ 99 02	3 yrly + Last	3 yrly + Last	Company	1450	Class 1		I E R	I E R					T I E			
1A West Street, Norwich Contact: (Name)	20 yrs 6/87–6/07	~~£6,000~~ ~~£9,000~~ £10,000	~~91~~ ~~95~~ 99 02	5 yrly + Last	5 yrly + Last	Company	950	Class 1	I E	R	R		I E R					I E T	

Notes:

1. All the primary obligations can be shown as well as rights, e.g. to exercise an option to break. As each item passes (e.g. rent reviews are agreed), they can be deleted and a new figure inserted (if applicable). This will provide not only an updated, 'at a glance' record, but also a history of the property.

2. Using the calendar not only highlights timing for action but also (as here) concentrates the attention on the fact that all these properties terminate within two years of each other. Although the grant of a new lease is usual, it is by no means certain.

3. The calendar dates show that in 1998, 2001 and 2004 there is no property expenditure required, thus the results for those years will not bear their fair proportion of the costs of occupation. This can be overcome by creating a reserve for repairs (and possible dilapidations) by means of an annual charge. The reserve can then be drawn upon for the costs when incurred.

4. The abbreviations used in this are: I = internal redecoration, E = external redecoration, O = option (two-way), [O] = option (one-way), R = rent review, T = termination of lease.

The visual nature of the chart opposite highlights the fact that four of this organisation's main trading properties terminate within a two-year period. Although it may be unlikely that the landlords of those premises would all successfully oppose the grant of new leases, should they do this the organisation would be left with no trading premises. However, this could also be viewed as an opportunity. If, for example, the organisation had traditionally traded in this way but wished in future to trade from one main location and simply supply local requirements, the possibility of release from obligations in four existing premises within a short period could be attractive. Indeed, if there were a property boom at the time it might even be possible to commission a new central location, vacate two properties as their leases terminate and to try to assign the others and possibly gain a premium. The exposure should the assignees default will be relatively small but, if this is a concern, subletting could be considered.

Rating

Introduction

Income to fund UK local authorities is derived from central government, from occupiers of domestic property (via the Community Charge) and from occupiers/owners of commercial property situated within the boundary of an authority (via rates). The Community Charge is set by each authority and is a personal tax, whilst the rates on commercial premises are calculated by reference to rateable values of individual properties multiplied by a uniform business rate (UBR) introduced originally in 1990 at a rate of 34.8p and increased by the government annually in accordance with the movement of the Retail Price Index except at the time of a revaluation.

Rateable value (RV)

The Valuation Offices of the Inland Revenue are responsible for assessing the RV of every commercial property. The RV equates roughly to the open market rental value of the property, although it does not usually equal it. The physical collation of all RVs becomes the Rating List. In order to avoid having to revalue every commercial building each year, the RV for new or altered buildings is determined by reference to the valuations of similar properties forming part of the existing rating list. This reference to the 'datum' level of rental values is referred to as the 'Tone' of the Rating list.

Rateable revaluations are carried out every five years usually resulting in an upwards movement. As a result of the slump in demand for property in the early 1990s the 1995 revaluation showed some substantial reductions from the 1990 figures which were when the most recent property boom was still having an effect.

Amount due calculation

From the Inland Revenue list, each authority extracts the RV for the properties in its area. Under the old system of rate calculation the Authority divided the amount of revenue it needed to raise from the occupiers of business premises in its area by the total of the rateable values RVs and arrived at a 'rate in the £'. Under the system introduced in 1990 in England

and Wales in 1990, (the system for Scotland having been introduced earlier), a uniform business rate (UBR) was established by central government and commercial rates paid became the product of the new RV multiplied by the UBR.

Central Government's intentions

The Conservative government at the time stated that it intended to increase the UBR and thus the costs of rates by no more than the annual rate of inflation. However, the effect on an individual commercial occupier has varied widely as a result of the five-yearly rating revaluation. Following the 1990 revaluation rates costs for commercial properties in the south of the country rose to a far greater extent than costs for properties in the north, whilst rates costs for office and retail premises rose generally to a greater extent than costs for warehouse and factory premises. Conversely in the 1995 revaluation which followed the general slump in property values, many rateable values in the south showed a reduction which was not duplicated in the north.

Transitional relief

To offset the impact of the increased costs in 1990, transitional relief was available to occupiers in residence before 1 April 1990, which effectively spread the increase over a five-year period. Similarly, in 1995 any occupier with a potential large saving had the effect limited by the same phasing concept.

There are special arrangements giving relief to small businesses and individual application should be made to the local office.

Appeals

Under the previous rating system, the appeal process could be (and often was) used as a device for delaying payment since as soon as an appeal was lodged, rates did not need to be paid. Under the new system appeals can only be lodged in special circumstances with a Valuation and Community Charge Tribunal (VCGT) whilst in the meantime the rates stated as being due must still be paid. If there is any reduction, so that an overpayment has been made, repayment will be made subsequently.

An appeal can be lodged under the following circumstances:

(a) if there is a change of occupation, and the assessment has not previously been tested by a Valuation and Community Charge Tribunal

(b) if there is a change in the property or its surroundings (e.g. if there is considerable rebuilding or redevelopment in an adjoining building),

(c) following the issue of a Notice of Alteration by the Inland Revenue Valuation Office altering the RV. In this case an appeal must be lodged within 28 days,

(d) following a decision of a Valuation Office on an appeal concerning a property which affects the RV of the subject property,

(e) if the assessment refers to a single occupation and is occupied in parts (or vice versa).

Rating appeals can be complicated as there are strict procedures to be observed and expert assistance should be sought. A number of organisations offer such a service, often on a 'no advantage, no fee' basis which can be attractive. However, the skill and experience of some such organisations is suspect and it may be better to use qualified surveyors who specialise in the matter.

First occupation

When occupying premises, rates become payable from the date when beneficial occupation commences for trading purposes. Authorities view 'occupation of part' as 'occupation of whole' and thus, if even only a small part of the new premises is occupied, rates may be payable from that moment on the entire property. The occupier should consider this rule when planning phased occupation, and will also need to confirm the effective date of occupation to the appropriate authority although some leeway may be obtained. Authorities can investigate instances of abuse.

Assessment of new premises

Following a notification of occupation, the authority requests the Inland Revenue Valuation Office to make an assessment, which may take several months. On receipt of the assessment, the occupier may appeal against it if they consider the proposed RV is not in accordance with the 'Tone' of the list.

Alternatively, within six months of occupation, and providing there has been no prior proposal, the occupier, being an interested party, has the right to make their own proposal. This should be served on the Valuation Officer who has six weeks to serve a counter notice stating if he considers it invalid. The occupier then has four weeks to appeal against the counter notice. If the Valuation Officer disagrees with a proposal then he must refer it to a VCGT within six months.

Empty property

During the property boom of the 1970s, some landlords developed the strategy of keeping property empty whilst rents climbed so that a better return could be obtained when the property was let. To counter this local authorities were able to charge double rates. This move was countered (particularly as the boom ended) by landlords removing the roofs of buildings so that they were unusable and therefore rates could not be levied on them. In most instances local authorities will not charge rates where a property is vacant. However, rates are chargeable from the moment the property is 'occupied' (which may be taken from the moment any furniture or machinery is installed).

In the case of *Hampson t/a Abbey Self Storage v Newcastle upon Tyne Council* it was held that the occupier of premises which, for rating purposes had been divided into seven different premises, did not have to pay rates on those premises (four out of the seven) for the periods during which they were 'non-occupied'.

For rates to be payable, four criteria must be satisfied:

(a) there must be actual occupation or possession

(b) there must be exclusive occupation for the particular purposes of the occupier

(c) possession must be of some value to the possessor

(d) possession must be for some period which is not transient.

Reinstatement

> **Introduction**
>
> Although most landlords will allow lessees to carry out alterations to their premises, usually this will be on a strictly controlled basis with the landlord requiring full details of plans, specifications, etc., and granting the right to carry out the work in a licence or deed of variation or similar legally binding agreement.

Regardless of the manner under which authority is granted for the works (it may even be possible to gain permission simply by the landlord signing and returning two copies of the plans covering the works), almost certainly the lessee will be obliged to undertake reinstatement at the termination of the lease.

Commitment

With a reinstatement clause or undertaking, it should be appreciated that there is a triple cost effect on the lessee as the following must be paid for:

(a) the original works

(b) the removal of those works under reinstatement provisions

(c) making good occasioned by the works being removed under the repairing obligations.

This may a question of cost but also of time since the landlord will require all works to be completed prior to the expiry of the lease which may have an effect on the lessee's occupation in the last few months of the term.

On some occasions of course, the landlord may prefer to leave the works in place as they may enhance the appeal of the premises to a new lessee. In such instances it may be possible to negotiate a financial deal whereby the lessee pays a sum to 'escape' the reinstatement liability. The amount will depend on the negotiations but anything which is less than the combined costs of reinstating and making good is likely to be advantageous, particularly as not only will the commitment be known but also the lessee will avoid the inconvenience of the building works taking place whilst they are in occupation.

> **Warning** When taking an assignment of a lease the situation regarding lessee's works, and reinstatement in respect thereof, needs to be checked to ensure the assignee either does not acquire an onerous liability or due allowance is made for the potential cost in the deed of assignment.

Relocation – General

> **Introduction**
>
> Planning and overseeing a relocation requires a considerable amount of thinking, planning, organising, arranging, talking and listening – all of which are time-consuming, require considerable attention to detail, and are very costly. It is not a job to be either allocated or taken on lightly and experience indicates that the task is usually underestimated resulting in difficulties, dislocation and a delayed new site start-up.

The successful project leader will need:

(a time to consider the whole project.

(b) time to consider how to lay out a new location.

(c) time to communicate with all involved.

(d) time to liaise with all the external agencies who may be or who have a right to be involved.

(e) time to take advice on employment law liabilities of employees on relocation.

(f) time to plan the move – which itself may be complex depending on the amount of production or computer-linked facilities which are to be relocated or the distance between the old and new locations.

(g) time to check that all facilities now existing will be replicated at the new location.

Reasons for relocating

There are many reasons why an organisation may need to relocate and an assessment of such reasons can help in developing criteria that must be met by the new location. The following are the main reasons put forward in a survey in the early 1990s:

(a) poor accommodation and facilities

(b) revision of business strategy and plans

(c) accommodation costs

(d) combination of these and other, less important, considerations.

In fact, most organisations move because of the combined effects of deficiencies at current locations rather than a single defect and because of the defects of existing premises rather than the attraction of new premises. In other words, most organisations were forced to move which often meant that the process was conducted under pressure and with insufficient time.

Location criteria

Before seeking a new location, the exact requirements need to be delineated. The following are examples of the initial criteria used by two organisations contemplating relocation searches.

Example A

- 30,000 sq ft
- good eaves height
- parking area
- room for expansion
- public transport access
- within 2/3 mile radius of head office
- trunk road access
- residential area
- good delivery access
- light and spacious conditions
- part-time staff available

Example B

Initial requirements
- flat green field site
- freehold
- power supplies
- minimum 35 acres (preferably 40)
- no manufacturing neighbours
- high water purity

Detailed requirements
- good communication links (export outlets)
- reasonable access of existing company distribution centre
- good access to international airport
- assistance/grants available (see below)
- component vendors locally

Labour requirements
- availability with bias to youth
- skilled mechanical and electrical technicians available

- availability of training establishments
- good industrial relations record of location
- good supply of local housing
- possible local authority assistance

Note In relocation example B the search was carried out for an organisation from the Far East. The search covered the UK, the Netherlands and Germany. A site in the UK was chosen mainly because there was a preference for an English-speaking workforce. This was a major factor which, despite a considerable amount of thought, was overlooked in the original list, demonstrating how essential it is to consider requirements from all angles.

Other considerations

If the raw material being used is heavy/bulky and the finished product is small/light it may be cost-effective to move nearer the raw material supply. If the reverse is true, it may be better to move nearer the market.

The value of the services on which the organisation draws in its current location should not be overlooked. They may only supply minor items but sometimes production lines can be halted for want of one customised bolt.

The relocation team

An early decision should concern whether to use internal or external sources for the project leader and the following matrix may aid decision-making on this point.

Internal	External
Advantages	
control, rapport, inexpensive, knowledge of organisation	objective, experience, skill, wider market knowledge
Disadvantages	
additional responsibilities, insular outlook, bias, inexperience	time needed to learn company ethos, practices, etc., additional charges

In controlling a move of any size the team may best be split into two – an external team dealing with the sourcing, acquiring and setting up of the new location (which could include the project leader, administrative support, architect, engineer, quantity surveyor, builder, secretary) and an internal team dealing with the requirements of personnel and processes required to move (which could include the project leader, administrative support, production and office representatives, communications, finance and personnel managers, secretary). The fact that the project leader, administrative support and the secretary are part of both teams should provide continuity and linkage between these different but interlinked functions.

If minutes of the meetings of both teams with named person 'action required' lists are distributed widely everyone should be kept informed of progress and problems. Depending upon the complexity of the move and the timescale, these team meetings may need to be held monthly, fortnightly or weekly, and the intervals may well shorten as the project nears completion, with virtual daily updates as the move date itself becomes imminent.

Communication

It is vital to keep everyone involved informed at all times including:

(a) telling employees what is going on.

(b) explaining what it means to them.

(c) giving information about the new location.

(d) arranging tours of the premises and surrounding area.

It is also essential that well in advance of discussion with or communication of the decision to the employee, the organisation decides its relocation assistance package (refer to RELOCATION – PERSONNEL). Specific advice may need to be taken on this if experienced personnel staff are not available in-house.

In addition, the need to keep suppliers and customers aware of developments – if only to reassure them regarding future business and supplies – should not be overlooked. It may also be necessary to advise them regarding any suspension of supplies or redirection of deliveries.

Support services

Relocation is not just about moving people and processes, i.e. machinery and machine minders. Also to be considered are the support services, offices, canteen, reception, as well as stocks and stores, records and record containers. Raw materials should be run down prior to the move with later deliveries made to the new site. This may entail installing goods inwards and security staff at an early stage at the new location.

> **WARNING** It is often the case that the immense effort and time needed to plan and effect a relocation are overlooked. The following checklist attempts to highlight the main areas of concern collated as a result of a survey of a number of moves.

Relocation considerations

(a) Dilution of management attention on the move can create problems with control of the business.

(b) There is a considerable advantage in having a person (possibly an outsider) who is able to concentrate on the project without the distractions of in-company responsibilities.

(c) It can also be very helpful to use someone who has had prior experience of a major move.

(d) An impending move can have an impact on staff morale and thus output. Good communication is essential.

(e) Sometimes the need to keep the decision process confidential creates problems among managers who want to take key staff into their confidence and to gain their input.

(f) Moving from north to south or south to north creates problems. Those asked to move from south to north may be worried about whether they could afford to move back into the southern England housing market; those moving from north to south may foresee a reduction in their current disposable income and a lowering of their standard of living.

(g) By far the greatest problems encountered in moving are delays. Usually unforeseen, these tend to be mainly related to the provision of new accommodation, i.e. building works, and the supply of specialist plant and equipment. Whilst individual delays can be countered, the domino effect – earlier delays causing increasing delays in later stages can enhance the overall length of the delay.

Post-relocation checks

Ideally the relocation team should be kept in operation in order to provide back-up and problem-solving facilities whilst the new location and staff settle down. The aim in the first weeks post-move is to recover the pre-move output figures and then to move smoothly past those figures. The fact that those responsible for the move are seen to be available may provide valuable moral support.

The old site

Finally, it is essential that the old site, if not disposed of at the time, is not forgotten. If left unoccupied it will need security and repair protection until disposed of.

Financial assistance

Under the Local Government, Planning and Land Act 1980 the Secretary of State for the Environment can designate areas of the country as Enterprise Zones. As well as the fact that relaxed planning rules apply in the (currently 81) zones, 100% capital allowances are available for industrial and commercial buildings for the ten years during which each zone can exist.

Under the DTI Enterprise Initiative there are three types of regional assistance, as listed below.

(a) a Project Grant based on the fixed cost of a project and on the number of jobs the project is expected to create or protect

(b) a Training grant

(c) Exchange Risk Guarantees (which covers borrowers in the UK against exchange risk on foreign currency loans from the European Coal and Steel Community).

Grants may also be obtainable from the European Union.

Relocation – Personnel

Introduction

It has been calculated that, on average, businesses move once every 12 years. Whilst relocating the operation requires a considerable amount of detailed planning to find alternative premises and arrange acquisition, fitting out and occupation, such essential work pales into insignificance compared to the problems that arise in attempting to relocate employees.

WARNING

1. Before attempting to require an employee to relocate (as opposed to inviting relocation), the exact wording of the employee's contract must be checked. Some contracts include a flexibility of location clause but even these do not give the employer complete freedom. The employer must be seen to act reasonably in terms of timing, distance, etc., in requesting a move. There have been a number of tribunal cases recently, some of which are subject to appeal, and the situation is unclear. In the *Meade-Hill and anor. v The British Council* case, the Court of Appeal found that the imposition of a mobility clause into a married woman's contract was discriminatory. The ruling was made on the grounds that more women than men are secondary wage-earners and thus would be more unlikely to be able to comply with the requirement. The employers were told the clause would be unenforceable unless it could be shown to be justifiable on grounds other than sex.

2. If the employee is required to work abroad then, under the Trade Union Reform and Employment Rights Act 1993, leaving the UK he or she must be given written particulars of:

(a) the term of the posting.

(b) the currency in which the salary will be paid.

(c) details of all additional benefits applicable.

(d) the terms and conditions governing the return to work in the UK.

Specific advice should be take on both the above points.

Procedure

The following procedure suggests action to cover all aspects of the problem.

A. Notice

At least three month's notice of the intention to relocate will be given in writing to those affected. Employees will be told they will be required to work at the new location (i.e. because their contract requires this - see Warning above) or whether they may work there if they wish, or that they are not required to move. Employees will be requested to confirm in writing whether they are interested in relocating within one month from the date of the letter of notice of relocation. When confirming their interest, they will also be required to confirm that they have placed their existing property on the market at a figure recommended by a local agent, or, if occupying leased property, that they have given appropriate notice, and that they have registered their housing requirement with a named agent at the new location.

B. Location Inspection

During the month after the notification of the relocation, visits to the new location and its surrounding area will be arranged for all employees considering relocating. Such visits will be supplemented by written data on the area and by interviews with local estate agents, schools, etc. The intention of these visits will be to give those relocating enough information to enable them to make a decision, which it is appreciated can have far-reaching implications for employees and their families.

C. Specific Notice

Once a decision has been made whether or not to relocate, a further letter will be given to the employee. This will contain details either of the relocation package offered, or of the alternative, which will usually, but not always, be the redundancy terms available.

D. Relocation Package

The relocation package, assuming the new domestic home location is within [say, five] miles of the new organisation location, will be fully applicable, provided the new residence mirrors the facilities available at the existing location. Should the employee wish to acquire a property with improved facilities or of a greater size, or a greater distance from the new location, the amount payable under this package will be restricted. The intent is to allow employees to acquire a similar property to that currently occupied, and a similar or shorter distance from the company facility.

The package includes reimbursement of:

(a) the costs (including agent's and solicitor's fees) of selling an existing property or vacating leased premises.

(b) the costs of packing and moving possessions (including any short-term storage involved).

(c) any costs involved in purchasing or leasing the new property.

(d) a [free] bridging loan from the organisation for a period of 3 months during the sale of the existing property and the purchase of the new property.

(e) travel and incidental expenses incurred in visiting the new area and inspecting accommodation and schools.

All invoices included in items (a) to (c) above must be made out in the name of the organisation, and will be settled by it.

> *Note*   This should enable the company to reclaim VAT incurred, although detailed advice may be needed to ensure this is the case.

Employers (and employees) should note that currently the Inland Revenue tax-free limit for relocation expenses is £8,000. Although gross amounts will be paid by the company, these amounts will be subsequently declared on Form P11D and tax may be charged on them.

E. Clawback

Should an employee, having been relocated, and having received a relocation package, then leave the organisation voluntarily, any relocation allowances will be repayable as follows (example only)

(a) leaving within 3 months of relocation: 100% repayment

(b) over 3 months and up to 1 year: 80% repayment

(c) over 1 year and up to 18 months : 60% repayment

(d) over 18 months and up to 2 years: 40% repayment

(e) over 2 years and up to 3 years: 20% repayment.

F. House Sale Difficulties

In the event that the bridging loan facility has been exhausted, but the former residence has not been sold, and seems to have no likelihood of being sold, the employee will be required to sell the property to a company nominated by the organisation, and to liquidate the bridging loan. In the event that the then vendor sells the property at a figure in excess of its offered price, it is usual for the employee to receive a share of this excess. If the property is subsequently sold for less than the price paid to the employee the difference may be treated as a taxable benefit in the hands of the employee.

> <u>Note</u> *Advice should be taken on the taxation implications of such an arrangement, and the effect on the place of work now required to be stated in contracts of employment by the Trade Union and Employment Rights Act 1993.*

Rent – Confidentially Agreements

> **Introduction**
>
> Should the lessee gain a particularly good deal when rent is agreed at review, or even on grant or renewal of a lease, the landlord may stipulate that they will agree the rent only if the lessee does not disclose the figure agreed to any third party.

Purpose

The point of requiring a lessee not to disclose the rent they are paying is to protect the rental levels of other properties that the landlord may own and lease in the immediate neighbourhood. If the rent is lower in the subject property than elsewhere, come review time in the other properties, the lower rent could be used by other lessees to mitigate a rise in their rent at the time of review.

Evidence

To evidence the binding nature of such an agreement landlords will usually require the lessee to sign an undertaking that they will not disclose the rent they are paying, and that if they do any concession may be brought to an end. In many ways the mere existence of a confidentiality agreement itself should indicate to an enquirer that a deal advantageous to the lessee has probably been concluded. This may be so but can hardly be used as evidence. Indeed, the landlord may wish to incorporate in the agreement the requirement that in answer to any query, the lessee must state that it is not their policy to disclose property occupation costs to outsiders.

Named lessee concession

Often a concessionary rent agreed in this way, whether evidenced by an agreement or not, is restricted to the occupation of the premises by the named lessee. Thus, in this instance, if the lessee wishes to assign the lease, a new non-concessionary rent must be agreed that will be applied to the new lessee.

Summary

Generally, rent confidentiality agreements are disliked by lessees and those acting for them as they distort market rents and make the sourcing of comparable evidence more difficult.

Rent – Paying and Collecting

Introduction

The prime principle behind occupation of premises in the ownership of some other party is the need to pay the charge for that right of occupation. The manner in which such rent is to be paid should be set out in the document conferring the right of occupation. For leases and licences issued since the early 1970s (and in some cases before then), late payment of rent usually attracts an interest charge as well as being a breach of the lease covenants.

Payment principle

Rent is due on set days. Usually these are the four quarter days – in England and Wales 25 March, 24 June, 29 September and 25 December, and in Scotland, 2 February, 15 May, 1 August and 11 November – although the exact dates set out in the lease should be noted as these can vary according to region, custom, etc. Rent may also be deemed to be due whether demanded or not, so non-receipt of a rent demand would not be a satisfactory reason for non-payment and the resultant late payment would attract penalties (if any) in the lease.

There is nothing to stop rent being paid in advance of the due date and in some cases (for example, with a lessee whose financial strength is suspect) a landlord might insist on being paid (say) a year's rent in advance.

Conversely, during the recession a number of businesses successfully negotiated payment of rent monthly in arrears to assist with cash flow problems. There is no need for a landlord to agree to such a request if the lease stipulates rent being paid quarterly in advance, but in such circumstances it is perhaps better that rent is paid on a delayed basis than not paid at all.

Payment methods

Rent will usually be accepted by any reasonable means although by cheque is the most normal. Increasingly lessees are coming under pressure to pay either by banker's order or by direct debit thus allowing the landlord access to their bank account for collection of the rent (and other monies) due. It is understandable if some lessees object to this manner of payment and it depends on the strength of each party's hand when the lease terms are being negotiated.

The concept of issuing post-dated cheques may be best avoided. Banks are under no obligation to respect the post-dating of a cheque and thus if such a cheque is paid in, the bank may honour it. Should there be insufficient funds in the accounts, this could have a number of repercussions ranging from a minor cash flow effect, through the incurring of penal charges for operating an unauthorised overdraft to the potentially serious situation of the cheque being 'referred to drawer' thus raising questions of the lessee's financial standing. Meanwhile, the landlord will have the benefit of the money.

Collection

As far as the landlord is concerned, prompt settlement of rent is not only a basic requirement of the contract set out in the lease but is also a commercial necessity. Accordingly, the fact that 'rent is due on a certain date and delays are unacceptable and treated seriously' is a philosophy which needs to be brought home to each and every lessee. Other than setting out the requirements (and the penalties) in the lease itself (where it may tend to be overlooked because of the legal terminology and the length of the lease lessees need to have their attention drawn to the point at the appropriate time – i.e. before the first payment of rent is due. Thus a letter such as the following may serve both as initial advice that rent is due on a particular day and also as an indication of the landlord's action should rent not be paid promptly.

Dear

Address

As you are aware you hold a lease of the above premises from us. An annual amount of [£Sum] rent is due under that lease in four equal payments, the first of which amounting to [£Quarter's rent] is payable on [date]. We should be obliged if you would arrange to send us your cheque for this amount to arrive at these premises by [date being the date due].

RENT — PAYING AND COLLECTING

> *Note*   *The first payment may be in respect of a split period and thus it may be necessary to explain the way in which the rent due has been calculated. There will be a variance if rent is calculated on a daily basis (annual rent divided by 365) or as a proportion of a quarter (annual rent divided by four and then divided by the number of days in the quarter).*

It may help if we set out the administrative arrangements for the collection of future rent.

Two weeks before each quarter day, we will send you a rent demand so that you can process it for payment on or before the due date.

We feel sure you will not object to us reminding you that since late payment is a breach of the covenants contained in the lease, we take any delay in payment of rent extremely seriously.

As stated in the rent demand, rent is due on the dates stated, whether demanded or not. This rent demand is issued as a courtesy and no reminder will be issued. Should rent not be received on or before the date that it is due, it is our policy to place collection with our solicitors whose charges (and any charges incurred as a result of any court action), will be raised on to the lessee. Interest at [state rate in lease] will be added in respect of any late payment. Such interest payments are due within seven days of notification and again no reminder to pay will be issued. Should there be any reason why rent cannot be paid, please contact this organisation in case we can be of assistance.

Yours faithfully/sincerely

Rent demand

In addition, a rent demand such as the following could be used.

Name and address of organisation

Name, (address, if different from above) and telephone number of person responsible for property rental collection.

RENT DEMAND

Date

To (name and address of tenant)

Property (address)

The following amounts are due in respect of the item(s) shown.

Rent for period [dates]	[amount]
Service charge [data – may also need supporting schedule; check lease requirements]	[amount]
Insurance [data]	[amount]
Other (e.g. interest due re late agreement of rent review, late payment of previous rent)	[amount]
TOTAL DUE ON [DATE]	

Please ensure your cheque/money transfer/cash is received by us by the due date.

[Name and position]

Please note:

(a) Rent is due on the dates stated, whether demanded or not. This rent demand is issued as a courtesy and no reminder will be issued.

(b) Should rent not be received on or before the date that it is due, it is our policy to place collection with our solicitors whose charges (and any charges incurred as a result of any court action), will be passed on to the lessee.

(c) Interest at [state rate in lease] will be added in respect of any late payment. Such interest payments are due within seven days of notification and again no reminder to pay will be issued.

> *Note* This demand enables other charges due under the lease to be collected at the same time as the rent (assuming this is allowed by the lease).

It should be stressed that in referring to the need to pay promptly the exact terms of the lease must be adhered to. Some (mainly older) leases allow seven or 14 days' grace for rent payment. Not only must this time be allowed but also interest could not be charged until the 15th day.

Consistency

The above preparations should set the scene for the procedure to be followed by the landlord. However, unless the procedure is adhered to in practice, then the policy will fall into disrepute. Accordingly, late payment must be referred to the solicitors even if their charges are waived on the first occasion. The knowledge that the organisation will police the payment procedure forcefully will help underline the need for prompt payment.

Rent-Free Periods

Introduction

Agreement to occupy premises, even where the landlord, or their advisors, wish to use a standard form of lease, is a process of negotiation, with the terms of trade weighted in favour of one party or the other. This depends on individual matters as well as on the strength of the property market on both a national and local basis. To acquire a dependable lessee (one that is referred to as being 'of good covenant'), a landlord might well be prepared to ask slightly lower rent than would be asked of a new business or one that is perceived to be of high risk. Alternatively, the fact that a property has been empty for some time and/or is in a poor state might also be a sound reason for offering inducements to complete. One such inducement is a rent free period.

Principle

Under a rent-free arrangement, the lessee has the right of occupation but the landlord waives the obligation on them to pay rent for a set period. This is a particularly convenient way of 'giving funds' to the lessee where, for example, the premises are in a poor state of repair and the lease places repairing obligations on the lessee or where the lessee will need some time to customise the premises for their occupation.

Rent-free periods should always be evidenced in writing to avoid both immediate and later arguments concerning the amount of time for which the allowance was given.

Timing

Although it is more usual to find a rent-free period being allowed at the commencement of the lease term (mainly since the reasons for it being given tend to relate to initial occupation), it is not unknown for similar periods to be allowed during the term if, for example, the premises are affected by any landlord's works.

Valuation

If it can be proved that the period was given as an inducement to occupy because, for example, the premises had been empty for some time, then lessees of surrounding premises may be able to argue at the time of a rent review that their rents should be less than that otherwise asked. For example, if the passing rent for a property was £20,000 but a landlord allowed a year's rent free occupation, the actual amount of rent that will be paid until the next review in a normal five yearly reviewing lease would be £80,000. If that figure is then spread over the whole five year period, it is arguable that the real annual rent paid by that lessee is effectively £16,000 and this should be taken as evidence. Although the logic may be sound, the full effect of the rent-free period in this example would not always be agreed. As always, it comes down to a process of negotiation (see RENT REVIEW).

Rent Review

Introduction

The concept of rent being reviewed during a lease is mainly a post-war development and is a product of the inflation experienced during that period. In times of very low inflation, what would be considered by today's standards as extremely long leases – of 42, 63 or even 99 years – might be granted without review or at least with a review, not more frequently than, say, every 21 years. However, with inflation levels rising, landlords needed protection from the decreasing value of money and review patterns of 14, 7, 5 and even 3 years were introduced. Not only did this mean that the landlord's interests were protected, but it created a major business activity. Before or after the review dates the value of the passing rent needed to be assessed by both parties and a figure agreed between them or, in the event of disagreement, decided for them by a third party. Since in any one location most reviews occur on a random basis, knowledge of such reviews and movements is essential at review time.

Note *Throughout the following section it has been assumed that the landlord has initiated the action since it is anticipated that the rent will increase on review. Since the UK recession of the early 1990s, however, demand for property has fallen and so have some asking rents. In these circumstances, it cannot be assumed at the time of a review that a rent will rise. If there is no upwards-only clause (see below) and the lease allows it (which may be a consideration to be borne in mind when agreeing lease terms in future), it may be possible for a lessee to initiate the review process in the anticipation that they may be able to reduce the rent. The exact procedure must be adhered to where the lessee initiates the process, as for a landlord's review.*

Timing

Included in the lease will be guidance to the times when a review can be required by the landlord. Such clauses need to be carefully studied since they are not always accurate or comprehensive. Nonetheless, whatever they require should be effected (see below). In addition, any time limits must be understood. Clauses vary from applying strict time limits for the serving of notices and counter-notices, possibly (if time is stated to be 'of the essence') meaning that a review could be missed if the time limits are not observed, to being so loose that even though the review date has been passed a proper notice can be served and the review completed, with any uplift in the rent backdated to the review date. Alternatively, some clauses will allow the notice to be served well past the review date but stipulate that the increased rent will not be payable 'until agreed' (which provides a strong incentive for the lessee to try and delay agreement for as long as possible). The best advice is to ensure the review clause provisions are fully known and understood.

Basis for assessment

The bases on which the review must be agreed will usually be set out in the lease. Astute landlords will understandably endeavour to construct a basis for review which enables them to charge as much as possible. Conversely, lessees will wish to pay as little as possible and need to consider and, if necessary, argue against the review bases inserted in the lease at the time of negotiation. The most common bases often inserted in review clauses include the following:

(a) open market rent. This can be fair to both sides provided there are no restrictions in the lease which apply to the lessee. However, if there is a strict user clause, this could reduce the value of the open market rent for this lease were the property to be offered on the market since it could only appeal to a limited number of lessees who could comply with such a clause.

(b) vacant possession. In times of buoyant demand, unoccupied property may command a figure higher on the open market than it would with a lessee, particularly if any user clause is restrictive.

(c) length of lease unexpired. Whilst not a problem in the early years of the lease, the value of the lease to the lessee decreases as the unexpired term decreases. If the business is very much tied to the property position (e.g. in retailing) and there is a possibility that the lease will not be renewed, its value to the lessee can be severely reduced. If at review the lease requires the term to be considered as full even when there is only five years left the two parties could have a widely differing view of an appropriate rent.

(d) good state of repair. With a full repairing lease this should have an even effect on both parties. However, if the lessee does not have responsibility (or full responsibility) for repair, but the landlord does and does not comply, the lessee could be disadvantaged as rent would be based on the property being in a good state of repair when it is not.

> *Note* In the case of British Telecom v Sun Life Assurance, *the Court of Appeal held that where a term in a lease obliged the landlord to keep parts of the property not occupied by the lessee in good repair then the landlord is obliged to keep those premises in repair at all times (that is, the landlord could not have 'a reasonable time' within which the defect should be rectified, but needed to carry out the repairs immediately).*

(e) unrestricted assignment and underletting. Where assignment and underletting are allowed without restriction, then this is a reasonable basis. If, however, assignment and underletting are at the discretion of the landlord, or are not allowed, then stating that the review must be based as if there are unrestricted clauses would be manifestly unfair to the lessee who is effectively locked-in to the premises.

(f) lessee's occupation, goodwill and works. Stating that additional rent in respect of the lessee's occupation and goodwill should be ignored is fair to both sides. However, if a lessee's works are to be included in the valuation then that is decidedly disadvantageous to them since they will have paid for the works and could, at review, also be charged rent for the works if these have increased the value of the premises (see LESSEE'S WORKS).

(g) upwards-only reviews. During and following the property booms of the 1970s and 1980s, the concept of rents being reviewed only in an upwards direction came to be written into leases. Whilst this may be reasonable for any period during which property values are rising, when there is no boom – or even a slump – lessees can find themselves in difficulties. As trade declines, properties fall empty. The asking rents of these empty properties will tend to fall as landlords try to market them in low demand. Lessees locked into leases can find at review that they are already paying substantially more than a neighbouring property but, with an upwards-only review clause, can do little about it other than quote it as evidence that, at least, the rent should not be increased.

Upwards-only clauses distort property rents, act detrimentally against lessees and should be resisted. The UK government considered legislation during the early 1990s to ban upwards-only reviews but deferred this pending development of a code of practice by the property industry.

(h) floor areas. The actual usable area of the premises must be calculated accurately. This is particularly important with retail premises where zoning comes into play. Zoning means that the first 20 feet of depth from the pavement line is usually regarded as Zone A, the next 20 feet as Zone B and the remainder as Zone C. The area of Zone B is divided by two and of Zone C by four (or sometimes by six). The figures for B and C are added to the area of Zone A to get what is called a Zone A Equivalent (ZAE) as shown in the illustration below.

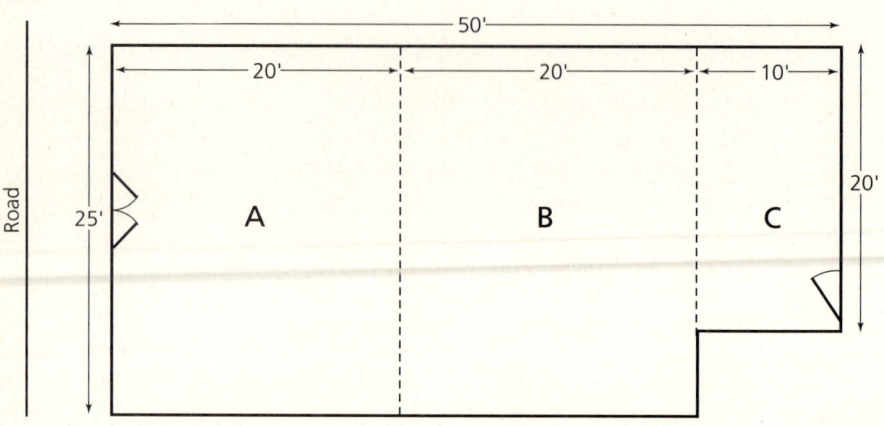

Zone A : 25 x 20 = 500

Zone B : 25 x 20 divided by 2 = 250

Zone C : 20 x 10 divided by 4 = 50

Zone A Equivalent   800 sq ft

If the current rent of this property is (say) £8,000 then the rental value of the ZAE is £10.

If the ZAE of a neighbour is valued at £20 then it could be argued (ignoring all other factors) that the rent of this property should be around £16,000.

The value of calculating a ZAE is that it enables the rents of properties of widely differing configurations to be compared.

In addition, of course, there may be storage and other areas which need to be valued although at a considerable discount to the main areas.

Offices are usually valued on a net internal floor area basis whilst industrial buildings are valued on a gross internal basis.

Regardless of the type of property the problem with floor areas is that no two people will measure the same floor area, in the same way or come to the same totals, so it is important to try to reach agreement on this at an early stage either by negotiation, by reference to previous review measurements or possibly by carrying out a joint measuring session. Conversely, arguing about the floor areas may be a valuable stalling device which can be used to 'wear down' the opposition with the purpose of winning concessions.

(i) Assumptions re rent review pattern. The lease may specify that the rent is determined on the review pattern in the lease, a formula that is reasonable to both sides. However, some leases specify that rent is to be determined without regard to the review pattern. This means that the calculation of the rent would be on the basis of the lease without review. Since such a lease would be very valuable to a tenant, this could have the effect of inflating the review figure.

> Note There have been a number of court cases on this and similar points and specific advice should be taken if there is such a wording in a lease.

Procedure

The manner in which the review is progressed should be laid down in the lease.

(a) This will usually commence with the landlord needing to serve a NOTICE, in which case the exact requirements of the lease as regards timing and service should be observed.

(b) Lessees are often required to serve a counter-notice. Again, the exact requirements should be observed. Some leases, for example, require lessees not only to respond but also to state the amount they are prepared to pay in which case great care should be taken not to suggest a higher figure than that which is reasonable.

> Note If time is 'of the essence', a lessee that does not respond as required to the landlord's notice may lose the right to challenge the landlord's figure.

(c) Assuming notices and counter notices have been served, the parties should agree the floor area and, if applicable, any zoning so that at least there is agreement concerning these points.

(d) The bases on which the rent is to be determined (as set out in the lease) may or may not be discussed. Since the review process is one of negotiation, it may be that these matters will not be mentioned initially but used as bargaining points if needed.

(e) Normally the landlord (or agents acting for them) will produce evidence that supports their contention that the rent should be increased. Such evidence should be a reflection of the current rental trend of comparable premises in the area. The evidence submitted may be selective, that is, any evidence which does not support the required increase will not be mentioned. There may also be an element of bluff involved in that salient features of the rents quoted may be suppressed. For example, rent of (say) £60,000 may be quoted for the property 'next door' but the fact that an inducement of 12 months' rent free was agreed may not be stated, neither will the fact that the next review is not for seven years as opposed to five which gives the lessee an advantage. Thus, whilst such evidence should be noted, it may need to be checked for accuracy and completeness.

(f) Evidence which negates the landlord's figures and supports the lessee's contention that the increase should be (normally) as small as possible needs to be collected and presented. This should be sourced, preferably from surveyors who have acted for other lessees in the neighbourhood since they will usually have available the exact terms agreed, particularly if these were agreed bearing in mind a number of factors. If not, then evidence should be sourced direct from other lessees who should be only too pleased to exchange details in order to unite against the landlord in order to achieve low rents. However, some lessees are very reticent about giving out such details and few really know the full basis of settlement. Nevertheless, even outline figures may assist and, after all, if one side has difficulty obtaining such figures so too may the other side.

In considering evidence like must be compared with like and careful inspection of evidence obtained is essential. For this reason, unless a lessee is experienced in property matters, it may be better to employ a trained and experience surveyor to argue the review. After all, it is not simply a question of an extra £10,000 on the rent for this year but, assuming a five year review pattern, of an extra £50,000 to the next review. In addition, that next review will commence from a higher base.

Obtaining evidence

Many lessees, when asked for details of agreements prefer to see something in writing rather than disclose information over the phone to a stranger or even during a personal visit. The following letter could be used as a draft.

RENT REVIEW

Name of organisation

Address of property under review

I am engaged in a rent review of my organisation's premises at the above address. We believe that it is important for all occupiers that rents out of line with market values should not be agreed, and it would be very helpful if you could confirm the details regarding the premises (address shown below) that you occupy. May I thank you for any assistance you can give. Needless to say, we are willing to provide you with evidence of our rent, etc., if and when your own property is subject to review. Should your review/renewal have been dealt with by advisers, I should be much obliged if you could pass this letter to them with your request to provide assistance.

PROPERTY ADDRESS ....

OCCUPIER ....

TENURE   : Freehold/Leasehold

Note   : If freehold, no further action is required.

LEASE TERM   : ....years from   /   /   to   /   /

USER CLAUSE   :

RENT-FREE PERIOD :
Please specify any period allowed at nil or reduced rent.

REVERSE PREMIUM : £
Please specify any amount paid as inducement to take new lease.

REVIEW PATTERN   : Reviews every   years

LAST REVIEW   :   /   /   RENT AGREED: £

OBLIGATIONS   : Insurance/Internal repair/External repair
                    (Please delete as applicable)

ACCOMMODATION : Self-contained shop/office/workshop/warehouse
                Shop/office/workshop/warehouse with shared entry
                Upper part/flat/storage/garage

SUBLETS   : £
Please give details including rent of any sublet.

DIMENSIONS   : Width   Length
A rough indication of all relevant dimensions would be helpful.

FLOOR AREAS	: Basement	Ground
	First	Second
	Other	
ZONING	: A B C	
AGREED ZONE A	: £	
OTHER FACTORS	: (Please specify any restrictions on use or other factors which could affect the rental valuation e.g. if Privity of Contract applies, if rent is subject to VAT, etc.).	

> <u>Note</u> A reverse premium is a sum of money paid by the landlord to a prospective lessee in order to encourage them to take a lease of the property.

Determination

With two sets of evidence the parties will try and agree a mutually acceptable compromise. The tone of this negotiation will depend very much on the aggressive or otherwise stance of the parties. Some landlords attempt to gain every advantage from the review process, some take a more long-term and pragmatic approach to it. Disagreement is perhaps inevitable since the parties have diametrically opposed viewpoints. If agreement is not possible, or not possible within any time limit laid down in the lease, then normally the landlord (and in some leases both parties) will have the right to arrange the appointment of a third party to determine the review.

The third party is usually appointed by the President of the Royal Institution of Chartered Surveyors (RICS) which lessees could be forgiven for thinking does not seem to be a particularly impartial body, although generally the professionalism with which most reviews are dealt should answer this criticism. However, what can be frustrating to lessees is that the RICS refuses to become involved in disputes regarding the appropriateness of the appointment itself. Leases generally require the parties to have reached a point where their negotiations have stalled, but landlords' applications to the RICS have been successfully made when no negotiations have actually taken place. Since, in any event, the lessee has to bear part of the cost of the third party appointment, such recourse without the courtesy of any negotiations can be frustrating to a lessee.

After application to the RICS, the office (one of three that the RICS has set up to deal with such applications) notifies both parties of their involvement and selects a chartered surveyor with knowledge of the area in which the property subject to review is located. If such an appointee is unacceptable to either party (for example, a lessee might not have a normal working relationship with a surveyor following an earlier dispute), it may be possible to object and for an alternative to be proposed.

Type of appointment

The nature of the third party should be set out in the lease. They can be either arbitrators or experts. Whereas an arbitrator essentially acts in accordance with the Arbitration Act and to some extent attempts to find a 'median' position fair to both parties based upon what the parties themselves say, an expert can rely on his/her own knowledge and expertise in addition to that put forward by the parties. Further, the arbitrator has powers to obtain documents by legal discovery, compel the attendance of witnesses and can hear evidence on oath.

The third party determines the format for arguing the case in writing with a timetable. The parties are expected to abide by the format and the timetable. They may be asked to attend a meeting to argue their cases or alternatively (and more likely) to make written RENT REVIEW SUBMISSIONS to the third party.

Having received the other party's submission, each has an opportunity – in a counter-submission – to argue against the contentions put forward. Although arguments against contentions can be made, the parties may not be allowed to introduce new evidence or facts at this stage. This will be laid down by the third party and should have the effect of forcing both parties to put forward their best case in the first submission.

Following receipt of the counter-submissions, the third party, who may have visited the property and the area, will make a decision regarding the level of the review and this will be made available when the parties have paid the third party's fees. If the third party is an arbitrator, the decision is an award; if an expert the decision is a determination.

Fees

The third party will charge for his or her services. This tends to be around 5% of the average between the parties' original rental estimates. Thus if the landlord stated their estimation of the reviewed rent was £40,000 but the lessee felt it should be £30,000, the total costs to be charged by the third party would be 5% of 50% of (£40,000 + £30,000) or £1,750. In addition, the third party's expenses and VAT on the whole sum must be paid.

Normally the parties will pay around 50% of the costs each. However, the third party can determine that one party should pay a greater proportion of the costs than the other. (This might be the case if it is felt than one party has not dealt with the review in a constructive manner or has been unreasonable, or has been guilty of delaying the process unnecessarily.) Since the parties will not know of any split of the costs until they read the determination it is usual for both parties to send the third party 50% of the total cost in order to obtain the decision, and then if there is any split other than the 50% to make an appropriate adjustment. Alternatively, the landlords, who will usually have requested the appointment, may pay the entire fee to obtain the decision and then recharge the lessee.

Confirmation

Once the review is determined – either by a third party or by the parties by negotiation between themselves – it should be evidenced in writing by means of a RENT REVIEW MEMORANDUM.

Effect

Once the rent is agreed, either by negotiation or by the third party issuing a decision, the amount determined becomes the rent required under the lease and must be paid (with any arrears and interest, if any) by the lessee.

Cost-effective approach

Rent can be a major factor of business expense and for this reason it may be entirely appropriate for a hard line to be taken by a lessee in trying to reduce a rental figure put forward by a landlord. For this reason pushing the determination to a third party may be logical. However, it must be realised that such determination is risky and the full effect of costs needs to be considered.

Case study

A lessee had a shop unit slightly off the main area of retail appeal which commanded proportionately higher rent. The landlord asked at review for a rent of £40,000 – a 100% increase – using the rents in the prime area as evidence. By negotiation this was reduced to £30,000 – a 50% increase. However, the lessee did not feel the rent should be more than £27,500 and believed they had evidence to support it and that the landlord had not given enough discount for the fact that the shop was not in a prime position. It was decided to resist to the point of third party determination, particularly as there was no interest payable in respect of a late agreement on review and the determination by a third party would take at least two months.

It was pointed out that to incur a third party determination a surveyor would be need to be appointed to prepare the submission and any counter-submission (fee plus expenses, say £1,300) and the lessee would also bear at least 50% of the costs of the third party. Since the lessee's opening submission would be £22,500 and it was estimated that the submission from the landlords would start at £35,000 this would cost (including expenses) around £1,500.

It was felt that for a one-off cost of around £2,800 it was worth forcing the point. In the event the third party was required to act as an expert. As a result of his own investigations, he discovered additional evidence that neither party had put forward and determined the rent at £30,000. In addition he determined that the lessee should pay 75% of his costs (possibly because the landlord had no way of recouping any interest on the additional rent).

This emphasises the risky nature of the process. Indeed, even had the expert accepted the lessee's assessment the first year's gain (£30,000 less £27,500) would have been virtually wiped out by the costs involved. The landlord might have accepted an offer of, say, £29,250.

WARNING: Surveyors keep records of the movements in rents generally and in particular areas. From their own personal contacts with others in the same profession, and with property directors and managers of large space-using organisations, they can easily source information (presented in the way they need it for comparison purposes) to aid them in negotiations.

Such information is not immediately available to the layman and conducting a rent review is a time-consuming undertaking. Further, if negotiations are protracted, as increasingly they tend to become, the situation in the immediate area of the property may alter. For a review lasting, say, six months, at least three visits may need to be made to the area to see what is happening nearby. If the person responsible is on site this is no problem but if the subject property is some distance away considerable time may be spent on these visits. Very few rent reviews can be conducted from a desk unless one has available the information

> available to surveyors. These factors need to be considered when considering whether to employ a surveyor or not, as well as the possibility of agreeing too high an increase through ignorance of other reviews and renewals. Saving a surveyor's fee may be false economy, particularly since the review agreed this time becomes the starting point next time round.

> <u>Note</u> When the lease is to be renewed a similar process of each side putting forward rental evidence is used. However, since the referral to the RICS is not appropriate, should the parties not be able to agree, recourse to the Court is necessary where the judge will decide the rent guided by an expert appointed for the purpose.

It is normal for the process of determination and renewal of a lease to be initiated by the landlord. However, at renewal, the protection of upwards-only rent reviews is lost. If rents are static (or even falling), landlords can protect their position by not seeking to determine the lease at all but simply letting it run on at the existing rent. In such a situation, the lessee should take steps to terminate the lease with the aim of being able to renegotiate the rent referring to open market evidence and without being hampered by the upwards only clause.

Rent Review Memorandum

Introduction

Whether a review is agreed during informal negotiations or is determined by a third party, it is normal for it to be evidenced by the completion of a Memorandum. If the rent at the figure agreed is submitted by the lessee and accepted by the landlord there may seem to be little point in having a memorandum of the new figure but it is in everyone's interests that there should be some document recording the agreement. Such evidence may be pertinent should one or other (or both) parties to the lease sell or assign their interest.

Format

The lease may stipulate a form of words to be used and if possible, the lessee should argue for this to be the case when agreeing lease terms originally. Some leases require the preparation of a memorandum by the landlord's solicitors and also require the lessee to pay for it. Given that the purpose of the review is (usually) to allow the landlord to collect an increased rent, it may seem iniquitous for the lessee to be asked to pay for the preparation of a document evidencing such an increase. All that is required is a simple form of words such as that shown in the draft set out below. Generally each side should bear their own legal costs (a principle set out in the Cost of Leases Act 1959). However very often this becomes a matter of negotiation.

MEMORANDUM dated .... to be attached to a LEASE

dated .... and made between ....

(the Landlord) and ....(the Lessee)

relating to the premises known as ....

By this memorandum dated ....199 , the Landlord and the Lessee hereby record that the rent payable under the lease has been reviewed pursuant to the terms thereof and fixed at [RENT IN WORDS] [RENT IN FIGURES] PER ANNUM exclusive payable from and including [DATE OF

213

REVIEW] until [DATE OF NEXT REVIEW, subject to further review as provided in the lease] or [DATE OF TERMINATION].

Signed by ....(the Lessee) in the presence of .... Witness

of (address and occupation) ....

....

Signed by ....(the Landlord) in the presence of ....Witness

of (address and occupation ....

....

Nil increase

With the surplus of property available following the recession, nil increases at review have become more common. Even though the rent continues unchanged it may be advisable for this to be stated in a memorandum, in which case the following wording might be used in substitution for part of the above draft.

Pursuant to and in accordance with the provisions of the lease dated [date] and made between [parties], [name of landlord] the landlord (being the present landlord of the property) and [name of lessee] the Lessee (being the present lessee of the property) have agreed and determined that the rent payable in respect of the property with effect from [date] being the date on which a review of the rent was due is to be [amount - which will be the same amount as that being paid in respect of the previous review period].

Signed, etc. (by both parties)

Rent Review Submissions

Introduction

Set out in RENT REVIEW is the procedure by which the parties to a lease can settle the rent on review – either between themselves informally or by reference to a third party more formally. To obtain a decision from a third party, it is necessary for submissions of evidence and ancillary facts and contentions in favour of one party's suggested figure and against the other party's to be put to the third party for a decision which will then become binding upon them.

Format

A submission takes the form of a document the content of which, together with a draft review (the essentials of which were used in an actual case), are set out below. Two copies will be required, since one is sent to the other party for comment. Submissions can be quite lengthy depending on the size and complexity of the property and the lease terms. It is probably wise for those who do not have sound experience of reviews and the implications of lease terms, even if they have argued the review to this point, they appoint a surveyor to prepare the submission and any counter-submission.

A submission normally contains details of:

(a) the experience of the person preparing it.

(b) the knowledge that person has of the area in which the property is located.

(c) a description of the property and the floor areas.

(d) details of the lease and the bases on which the review is required to be determined (i.e. what is, or is not, to be taken into account).

(e) details of the evidence that support the party's calculation of the rent suggested at review.

(f) details of contentions which argue against the acceptance of the evidence put forward by the other party.

(g) factors affecting the area (e.g. availability of property, developments and closures, road schemes, etc.).

Example

In the case concerning which the following submission was generated, the current rent was £6,000 and the landlord asked for nearly £12,000, later reduced to £10,000. Whilst negotiations continued over several months, the lessee was unable to make headway in reducing the rent increase to what they considered was a reasonable level. Not only was the review – of a small shop in a somewhat run-down suburb of Bristol – being argued during the retailing and general property recession of the early 1990s, but also the location of the property was causing considerable concern as was highlighted in the submission. In view of the Landlord's intransigence a third party referral was generated. In fact the third party made an award of £7,000 which was less than the lessee had offered during the negotiations. In addition the lessee was required to pay only one-third of the fees and costs of the third party.

Rent review submission to [name and address of third party]

from [name, status and address of party making submission]

Re : [Address]

Experience
As a [professional qualification], I have been involved in property negotiation and administration for 20 years dealing with all aspects – acquisition, sales and leasebacks, disposals, lease negotiation, repairs and redecorations, rent reviews, renewals – for several property portfolios. These portfolios, ranging in turn from 30 to over 400 units, have included all kinds of property, large and small, single and multi-occupation and have included factories, warehouses, offices and shops.

Knowledge of location
My [organisation] has traded from the subject property [stated location] in a suburb of Bristol for over 20 years and we have [number] other units within a five mile radius of this location. We have considerable knowledge of trading conditions in the immediate and surrounding areas. The landlord acquired these premises only two years ago and the surveyor acting for him works in London. Whilst we do not question their knowledge and skills of property matters generally we do not feel that either have the same depth of knowledge concerning the property and the location as ourselves.

Local participation

The manager of this unit is well-known in the area and is a member of the local traders' association. As such he has detailed knowledge of trading conditions and has been involved in attempting to combat some of the security problems referred to later.

> *Note* *The points being made here are that an organisation situated in the area for 20 years should know far more about the actual trading conditions than newcomers to the area and those working over 100 miles away. In addition the fact that someone who works at the unit is involved in local activities and concerns should underpin this local knowledge claim.*
>
> *Obviously surveyors do travel the country and gain knowledge and form opinions of areas but they are unlikely to have such detailed on-site knowledge. Although the statement is made that property knowledge and skills are not questioned, this in fact may raise a question concerning such knowledge and skills in the mind of the third party!*

Situation and background

This unit is situated in a small, somewhat run-down parade in a depressed and violent area of Bristol. For some years the parade has been the target of repeated vandalism, riots and burglaries. As recently as [date], this unit was surrounded by a small mob, who uprooted a concrete bollard, threw it through the door of the unit and stole several thousand pounds' worth of products. This was the second burglary in two months suffered by the unit, and the [organisation] currently awaits the additional requirements and costs which will be demanded by insurers.

Bristol generally and this area in particular has been badly hit by the recession with unemployment running as high as 25% in places (*Financial Times* report of [date]). Sadly, Bristol and the surrounding area is a classic example of property stock being expanded to meet the demand of the mid and late 1980s, then being caught by the recession with an excess of both manufacturing and retail space, and an overlarge workforce. As just one example, it is estimated that up to 25% of the jobs in the Bristol area's defence-based industries are being and will be lost in the immediate future. Since the defence industry is a major employer in Bristol and the surrounding area this will inevitably have an impact on all trade in the area, with the poorer areas, such as this, suffering worst.

Staffing

The [organisation] has severe problems with the staff, who occupy the flat above the shop. This husband-and-wife team, who have tried their best to improve the profitability of the shop despite the problems cited above and increasing difficulties with shoplifting, and, as already stated have been involved with the local traders' association attempting among other things to improve the appeal and security of the location in general and this shop in particular, have requested that they be moved to another unit. Quite frankly, they are scared of remaining in such a difficult and frightening neighbourhood. They did not dare intervene in the burglary for fear of physical violence by the mob. If they leave we believe it will be very difficult to obtain replacements.

> *Note* *Whilst not entirely relevant to the strict requirements of information to be taken into account when considering a review, such information helps set the scene in the mind of the third party. In this case, the covering letter to the third party also suggested that if he cared to ring in advance, the manager of the shop would collect him from his office to avoid the third party having to park his car in the neighbourhood during his inspection!*

Rent Review

Under the terms of the lease a review was due [date], but, despite the lessee demonstrating to the landlord the very real difficulties of operating a unit in the above area at a reasonable return, the two parties have been unable to agree terms. There are no specific requirements regarding items to be taken into account in determining the review.

> *Note* *Set out in RENT REVIEW are the various bases which must be taken into account in determining the review. Each of these should be addressed in the submission to demonstrate whether or not it has any effect in considering the evidence submitted.*

Landlord's evidence

The landlord's agents' only evidence is a review agreed three years ago which seems to ignore the fact that since then the whole country in general and this area in particular has gone into the worst recession known, that most rentals have failed to increase and indeed, in many instances, have actually reduced.

The [organisation] has, as already stated, several units within a short distance of the subject unit as well as elsewhere in the southwest and throughout the UK. Most of these, fortunately, are located in better areas than this unit. A number of rent reviews have been agreed in recent months in such units and in every case the increase has been very limited (10 – 20%) and often the new rent has been implemented only under an incremental arrangement.

We cannot accept that evidence of a review prior to the current recession has any relevance now.

> *Note* *Strictly speaking, whilst they may be evidence of the general trend in property values, comments concerning other units are not strictly relevant. This review was perhaps somewhat unusual in that there was no current evidence and thus it was thought that assessment of the figure had to depend mainly on the 'appropriateness' of a settlement. The fact, as later referred to, that there was an empty unit next door, and that this unit had been empty for several months following the previous lessee absconding, was in many ways the most telling evidence. If the lease refers to open market rent then the fact that there are empty units with no interested prospective lessee should be persuasive evidence. With a vacant property the asking rent suggested in agent's particulars (which is usually a figure intended to be and understood by all to be a negotiable 'ball park' figure) may need to be discounted by say 10-20% (or more) for comparability purposes. This principle applies, to a greater or lesser extent to all properties but is particularly relevant to retail properties since empty units tend to reduce passing trade and demand for neighbouring units.*

Floor area

The measurements suggested by the landlord's agents, namely [detail], are agreed. We do not agree, however, their calculation of the Zone A Equivalent. Firstly, we cannot agree that ZAE is applicable to long narrow shops like this. Secondly, if we must use zoning as a guide, this should be on the basis, as widely adopted in previous reviews we have conducted, of a divisor of six rather than four on Zone C. Our calculation of the ZAE is thus [detail].

> *Note* *Zoning can be used by some as a form of straitjacket to be rigidly applied in all circumstances whereas its origination was solely to provide some means of comparability of units of widely differing configurations. The individuality of units needs to be recognised. Whilst the possibility of convincing the third party that a divisor of six should be used rather than the more usual four may be somewhat remote, at least it does provide another argument. Since the third party required only one submission (i.e. new evidence could not be put forward later), pre-emptive arguments were needed. In other words, the whole – and best – case needed to be made in one document.*

Evidence

No recent evidence has been forthcoming. The only evidence so far offered by the landlord to support the 100% increase in the rent they originally suggested is that of [neighbouring unit] which was reached on a private settlement three years ago at the height of the retail boom.

The fact that this rental was agreed by a lessee who was not represented indicates to us that the amount agreed was above the appropriate rental rate even at that time.

> Note   In putting figures forward as evidence, where a review has been agreed by a lessee who is not professionally represented, most surveyors will discount the rent agreed. The point is that without professional representation the lessee may save the fees payable to such an advisor, but may also agree a figure which is above the market rate, regarding this as a trade-off.
>
> Referring to the original request for 100% increase based on irrelevant evidence may suggest that the landlord has not approached the review constructively or fairly which in turn may help undermine the other party's reputation and contentions and help mitigate the split of the third party's fees.

During [date – several months previously], the [next door] shop ceased trading and thus the parade was further depressed by an empty unit. The landlords has been trying to let this unit ever since without success. They claim to have three interested users but still the shop remains empty as it was at the date of the review. It is arguable that if any agreement is now reached (which seems unlikely) it should be ignored as it postdates the review date.

> Note   In this instance the landlord's agents tried to bluff the lessee with repeated claims of having let the vacant unit to a number of new lessees. However on checking with the local agents, it was clear that there was no firm interest at all. Where reviews pass the review date, any later settlements may be ignored (whether increases or decreases). Having said that, if they are in favour of the party submitting the evidence it may be helpful to include them.

The importance of checking and rechecking the current position – and of visiting the unit and the area – cannot be overstressed, reviews cannot be argued from a desk.

Rental offer
In the light of the foregoing, we do not believe there is any justification for any increase in the current passing rent. However, since everyone anticipates that the economy will improve sometime in the future and the

review period covers the next five years, we are prepared to agree a review on an incremental basis commencing with a base of £6,200 for Year 1, £6,600 for Year 2, £7,000 for Year 3, £7,400 for Year 4 and £7,800 for Year 5.

Alternatively, we are prepared to agree a full review on the second anniversary of the last review [date] provided there is no increase until that date. This should provide an opportunity for the area to recover and, assuming the landlord can lease the property next door, to put forward some real rental evidence.

> *Note* *This is perhaps an unusual and innovative offer but one which seemed appropriate in the circumstances. It tried to both put forward an increase with which the lessee could live but also to show that despite there being no evidence the lessee was prepared to be flexible. In demonstrating this flexibility, the lessee was also trying to infer that the other side was being inflexible.*

[Signature]

Procedure

After completion, the submission (in duplicate) is required to be sent to the third party within a time-scale formerly set by them. The third party takes note of the two submissions and sends a copy of each to the other side. Depending on the instructions of the third party, the two parties may have an opportunity to put in a second submission or, more likely, can simply comment on the points made in the other side's submission. If the parties are required merely to comment it can be difficult to draw the line between comment and using new evidence to support such comments. In practical terms this may not be important but surveyors have been known to object to the other side using the 'comment' opportunity to put forward new evidence.

Once the second phase is completed the third party makes a decision and, once their fees and expenses have been paid, release their determination or award. The rent fixed becomes payable from the review date stated in the lease (i.e. the normal review date or, in accordance with lease requirements, a later date) together with interest if applicable. Normally the rent so determined will be required to be evidenced by both parties signing a RENT REVIEW MEMORANDUM.

Rental Evidence

Introduction

In RENT REVIEW, the question of sourcing evidence that will support the contentions of the parties as to the figure at which the rent should be fixed for the next review period is addressed. A draft letter is included which can be sent to neighbours. However, a lessee may not only send such letters but be in receipt of them.

Seeking evidence

Ideally, all rent levels would be known and the assessment of a review would be merely an arithmetical calculation. In reality much is not known, not least because of RENT CONFIDENTIALITY AGREEMENTS. Such imprecise knowledge provides an opportunity for either party to benefit from the other's lack of knowledge. Surveyors devote considerable time to updating their records of rent levels in general and in particular areas. One method of sourcing the information is by sending letters similar to the draft set out in the section on RENT REVIEW. If a lessee is in receipt of such a letter there can be a temptation to ignore and even dispose of it. However this may be very short-sighted since, if a lessee can provide information on a reciprocal basis, a source of information to be tapped at an appropriate time has been discovered. The letter and any reply should be placed with the file on the subject property and either used at the time of review to source information internally or passed to any professional adviser acting on the lessee's behalf.

Confidentiality

In addition to those who are bound by confidentiality agreements, some lessees are loathe to divulge details of the rent they are paying. Efforts may need to be made to convince them that there is little to be lost by the figure being known – and potentially much to be gained in terms of knowledge of local rent levels which are unlikely to worsen their position and may improve it.

Repairs and Redecorations

Introduction

Generally, lessees will be responsible for compliance with COVENANTS including those relating to the requirement to keep the leased premises in a good state of repair and redecoration. The sanction for not complying is the issue by the landlord of a SCHEDULE OF DILAPIDATIONS. Non-compliance with the schedule of dilapidations is not just a further breach of the lease which may lead to its forfeiture, but also gives the landlord the right to enter the premises, carry out the work and charge the lessee with the costs so incurred. In this event, these costs will almost certainly be greater than the costs that the lessee would have incurred, if only because the landlord will probably charge for the control of the works which would otherwise have been performed by the lessee.

Reasonable state

The fact that the premises must be brought to 'a reasonable state' – the wording used in most leases – does not necessarily mean that the state must be excellent, although there may well be difficulty in deciding what is 'reasonable', particularly if the building is old. After all, it is easier to keep a new building (erected with the benefit of new materials, etc.) in a good state of repair and redecoration than an old building. Accordingly standards of reasonableness may vary. If a Schedule of Dilapidations has been served then following the completion of the works, the landlord or his surveyor should be invited to inspect the works and then agree with the lessee and the contractor a list of those items which are not at the standard required (usually called a 'snagging list'). This may result in a certain amount of argument and/or negotiation, particularly if the lease is nearing the end of its term. In this case the landlord will want the property in good condition when handed back or made available for inspection by prospective lessees (assuming the current lessee does not intend renewing its occupation).

Materials

The materials used in carrying out the work should be of good standard but wording that appears in old leases such as 'paint with three coats of oil paint' should be challenged since modern materials remove the need for such multiple coats of paint. Indeed applying them could be counter-productive.

Frequency

Redecoration is normally required every three or five years externally and five or seven years internally. In addition, a final redecoration may be required in the last year of the term. Failure to comply with regular redecorations is widespread but may be shortsighted as landlords rely more and more on the use of Schedules of Dilapidations to gain compliance. Compliance with redecoration clauses may actually avoid needing to comply with far more onerous requirements that may be generated by the serving of a Schedule of Dilapidations.

Risk Assessment and Prevention

Introduction

Under current legislation, property occupiers are required to assess the risks that are related to their operation of the premises. Whilst these actions are required in relation to the safety of the workplace, the process is also very valuable related to the profitable operation of the business.

<u>Note</u> *Such an undertaking required under HEALTH AND SAFETY legislation has implications for the property, personnel, security, insurance and safety disciplines and to ensure a comprehensive approach involving all such disciplines in the assessment may be cost-effective.*

Risk survey

Purpose: To discover all aspects of risk which affect a particular department and/or division, in order to lead to an objective assessment of the impact value of those risks and their likely incidence.

Risk composition

The incidence of risk needs to be assessed and related to the operation of the business as follows. It will be necessary to identify:

(a) the various threats that can affect the operations, plant, facility and workforce as well as the process(es), raw materials and end product.

(b) resources available to the business through which its output is achieved.

(c) general and company-specific factors that increase or decrease the strength of the threat.

(d) the effect of the threat(s) if and when manifested.

Threats

List the various threats that could affect the achievement of the end product of each department. These may include:

(a) lack of raw material (interrupted supplies for a number of reasons – fire, strikes, transport delays, poor planning, etc.).

(b) lack of energy to process (fire, strikes, poor maintenance, lack of repairs, parts, etc.)

(c) lack of facility in which to process (fire, building collapse, lack of access, eviction, etc.).

(d) lack of demand for end product (collapse of market, fire, strike, next department cannot accept, etc.).

(e) extraneous factors (change of legislation, pollution problems, changing public demand, etc.).

(f) loss of records (particularly computerised systems).

Resources
For each area of the business for which a 'threat analysis' has been drawn up, identify those resources available to the business which enable the threat to be controlled, if not eradicated.

For example, several of the threats identified above relate to the department being part of a whole and thus needing to inter-relate to other departments (or external sources) to supply raw material and to accept the finished product. The problems that this operation will pose can be minimised by an efficient production control or production planning department. If this does not exist then these remain valid threats for that department.

Lack of energy to supply can be overcome by means of a stand-by generator and, if the department is critical to production, the company may need to consider installing such a back-up.

If the company is involved in a process that carries a high pollution factor it will need to monitor the implication of current and forthcoming controls (particularly legislation emanating from the European Union).

Summary
Having gone through this process for each part of the operation, management should have a detailed assessment of the risks, their quantification and likely incidence level. This report should be of immediate use in terms of risk prevention and reduction requirements and also in risk analysis and control.

Hazard identification and reporting

Under proposed European Union legislation it has been suggested that employees should have the right to withdraw their labour if they feel the workplace and/or process is unsafe. A limited right in this respect was introduced under the Trade Union Reform and Employment Rights Act 1993. It may be helpful to be proactive and encourage employees to report instances of danger or hazard so that the organisation has an opportunity to remove or reduce the hazard. One way of doing this is by using a hazard report form.

Organisation Name .... **Hazard Report Form**

To   : Safety Officer   From : ....

Date : ....   Safety Rep. for .... Area

Time : ....   Form number ....

Place :   ....

Please note that at the above time/place I became aware of what I consider to be an unsafe/unacceptable/dangerous/practice/machine/procedure/other (specify) (delete as necessary).

Comments/additional information ....

....

Signed ....   Date ....

Copies : Safety Committee, Works Manager

- -

Acknowledgement/Reply slip   No. ....

From : Safety Officer   To:

....

Date : ....   Time: ....

Thank you for bringing the details set out on this form to my attention. I am arranging to take the following action

Signed Safety Officer.................   Date ....

Copies : Safety Committee, Works Manager

Notes

1. Use of a self-carboning form will enable the reply to be given as part of

the report form whilst retaining the original for record purposes. Copies can automatically be given to the Safety Committee, Works Manager or other executive responsible for these matters, and the Company Secretary or executive responsible for property administration, risk management and insurance. etc.

(2) Numbering both halves of the form allows for ease of reference to the hazard and avoidance of misunderstanding as to which hazard has been actioned and which has not.

Risk prevention

Identifying risks is, of course, only part of the problem. The main challenge is to reduce or even eliminate the risks. Included in the following checklist are ideas for reducing risks to property and the workplace. The checklist is not exhaustive and is meant to be used only as a base for customised implementation.

Risk prevention checklist

Occupation risks

1. Ensure occupation rights are protected.
2. Ensure compliance with all covenants.
3. Keep repaired, redecorated and cleaned.

Security

4. Reduce entry ports.
5. Monitor remaining entrances/exits.
6. Utilise electric keys and/or door releases.
7. Change locks regularly (if the organisation has a number of premises it may be possible to exchange locks between them).
8. Use security passes instead of keys.
9. Improve / illuminate boundaries.
10. Link fire doors with intruder alarm.
11. Ensure that access to rear entrances remains anonymous.
12. Use dummy alarms.
13. Join Neighbourhood Watch.

RISK ASSESSMENT AND PREVENTION

14. Unexpected visits by management.
15. Eliminate or illuminate dark corners, etc.
16. Use anticlimb paint.
17. Protect windows and sensitive areas with grills and netting.
18. Appoint a person to take care of empty premises.
19. Utilise security sputniks and closed circuit television (CCTV).

Workplace

20. Ensure all systems reflect up-to-date legislation.
21. Ensure all landlords/insurers/inspectors recommendations implemented.
22. Ensure Fire/Evacuation drills carried out.
23. Systematically review controls.
24. Set up system of disaster analysis/contingency planning.
25. Use unguessable passwords in computer systems.
26. Monitor out of normal hours working.
27. Use incident folders to ensure all losses are known.

It should not be overlooked that this process tends to have immediate benefits in terms of better control and management.

Service charges

> **Introduction**
>
> Where a property is in sole occupation, responsibility for upkeep of the premises, repairs, redecoration, security, parking, etc. will usually be that of the lessee or occupier in accordance with the provision of the occupation authority (lease or licence). If, however, the premises are in multiple-occupation, it is usual for the cost of upkeep of common areas and of services which are provided for the benefit of all occupiers to be sourced centrally and for each occupier receiving benefit to contribute to such costs by means of a service charge.

Authority

In occupying premises which already have a service charge in operation there may be little a lessee can do other than ensuring

(a) that the proportion of the whole that they are required to pay is fair.

(b) that the items included in the charge are items from which the lessee derives a benefit.

> Note   It is not unknown for a lessee to be charged for the provision of items – for example, parking spaces – which they do not have.

If considering taking a new lease it may be possible to negotiate which items are to be charged and on what basis the apportionment is to be made. However, the landlord will have a list of items and costs and will be determined to recover these costs from the lessees.

Apportionment

If the demised premises are separately rated then the rateable value can be used as a basis for the determination of the proportion to be born by each lessee. Such an externally sourced value has the advantage of being independently assessed and recognised by all. It also reflects the fact that common parts allied to, say, a ground floor suite, may tend to have a higher value than those allied to, say, a fifth floor suite. However, the ground floor lessees could argue that they should not pay a proportion of the cost of maintaining a lift which they have no need to use and, if agreed, there may be some items for which a modified basis of charge may need to be used. If using the rateable value as a basis, care should be taken to ensure that the valuations are current and that none are subject to appeal or redetermination, or that the effects are to be taken account of when known. As an alternative base for assessment, floor area may also be logical.

Accuracy

It would be wise for lessees to request either that they inspect the contracts and/or invoices for the supply of the items included in the service charge or that there is provision for some independent authority to check the calculations and proportions and confirm to the lessees the accuracy of the charges. Often a firm of accountants is retained to do this.

Default

Charges are levied on the landlord who recoups the cost from all lessees. In the event that one or more lessee defaults on payment, the attitude of the remaining lessees should be that this is then a charge on the landlord and should not fall to be re-charged proportionately over the remaining lessees. Lessees will rarely have any control over who occupies the other areas in the property whereas the landlord does. Thus it is the landlord's responsibility to ensure collection.

Payment

In theory, payment for the services should become due after the services have been provided. In many modern leases, a deposit (often, a major part of the total expected) may be required to be paid, either a year in advance or sometimes in quarterly instalments with any balancing charge being collected once the final charges are known. Interest is sometimes stipulated to be added in the event of delayed payment of sums properly demanded. Whilst it may be possible to negotiate for the removal of such a clause, the logic is hard to dispute.

Complaints

The provision of services by an absent landlord to lessees is prone to problems of poor execution or even non-completion. A procedure needs to be set up so that lessees make notes of all failures to provide the services agreed, and of the manner and time of notification of non-performance.

Surveys

Introduction

During its existence, a property will be surveyed on a number of occasions for a number of different reasons. Owners and occupiers would be well advised to obtain copies of all surveys and lodge them with the records of the premises. Such surveys provide not just a record of the history of the property but also may provide valuable information for those required to inspect or survey the property at a later date. These surveys may also save later expense should, for example, funds be required using the property as security. Few lenders will provide funds without some idea of its state of repair. However, the borrower may be able to use an earlier survey for this purpose rather than commissioning a fresh survey which, with any sizable property, is likely to command a four figure sum. Even if the full fee cannot be saved it may be possible to negotiate a discounted concession by providing earlier details.

Types of survey

There are six main types of survey, as listed below.

1. Condition.

Before ACQUISITION, a prospective purchaser/occupier should always commission a full structural survey disclosing all and any work required to be done.

2. Insurance

Once acquisition has been agreed insurance cover should be obtained and effected from exchange of contracts. Insurers may well wish to inspect and report on the premises. Showing the insurance surveyor the condition survey may reduce the time required to be spent on this.

With leased premises, the landlord may require the property to be surveyed by his insurers. The lessee can request a copy of any report and should request that the interest of the lessee be endorsed on the policy.

3. Alteration

If work is to be carried out to the premises, a structural survey may be necessary. Earlier surveys may be of assistance in planning any such works.

4. Wants of repair

With leased property the lessee usually has a COVENANT to keep the premises in a good state of repair. If the landlord feels this covenant has not been complied with he can serve a SCHEDULE OF DILAPIDATIONS during the term of the lease. Until recently it was arguable that this can only be done when the interests of the landlord could be prejudiced by the non-repair. However, in the case of *Jervis v Harris* the Court of Appeal held that, despite the fact that by the end of the lease the property would not be standing (the outstanding term was around 900 years) the onus was still on the lessee to comply with the repairing covenants and that, in the event of failure, the landlord had the right of entry to the premises, to carry out the work and to recover the costs from the lessee.

In any event the lessee should keep copies of the schedule in case a further schedule is served. Satisfaction with work completed earlier may enable some items to be removed from a later schedule. (This may be particularly helpful should the landlord have changed.)

5. Survey with a view to sale or purchase

If a property is to be marketed, prospective purchasers will wish to know its state and will require a survey. This can pose problems since not only can it be disruptive to the occupier's business but the fact that the premises are for sale may be confidential and the occupier may not wish it to be known, particularly by employees who might, for example, be subsequently declared redundant. In this instance producing previous surveys may be sufficient to satisfy at least those whose interest is not firm in order to minimise such inconvenience.

6. Valuation

Owners of freehold property may wish to have the premises surveyed and valued regularly in order to arrive at a VALUATION figure which may be used within their financial records either as a balance sheet figure or simply as a reserve. Alternatively, a value might be sought where the possibility of a MARRIAGE OF INTERESTS is contemplated.

Tenancy agreement

> **Introduction**
>
> In order to maximise the return on an investment in property most owners will wish to ensure all parts of the premises are occupied. Such occupation may be effected under a range of legal instruments - UNDERLETTING, LICENCE and tenancy agreements. The latter arrangement takes the owner into the domestic letting area on which specific advice should be taken. The following tenancy agreements should be used as drafts only.

This tenancy agreement is made this [date] between [name and address of organisation] (hereinafter called 'the Landlord') of one part and [name and address of tenant] (hereinafter called 'the tenant') of the other part

WHEREBY IT IS AGREED as follows:

1. The Landlord shall let and the Tenant shall take ALL THAT [Description of property] (hereinafter called 'the demised premises' being part of the messuage known as [description of premises]

TO HOLD unto the Tenant from the [commencement date] from month to month at the weekly rent of [sum]

This tenancy shall be terminable by either party giving to the other of them at least one month's notice in writing expiring at the end of any calendar month

2. The tenant agrees with the Landlord as follows:

    i. To pay the rent at the times and in the manner aforesaid by bankers order and shall also pay all rates, council tax, taxes, assessments and demands which shall now or hereafter become payable in respect of the demised premises

    ii. To keep and occupy the demised premises for a private residence in one occupation only

    iii. Not to assign charge underlet or part with possession of the demised premises or any part thereof or to take in lodgers or paying guests

    iv. To permit the Landlord with or without workmen and others at convenient time in the daytime to enter upon the demised premises to examine the state and condition thereof and also for the purpose of repairing supporting and maintaining the building of which the demised premises form part and the sewers drains and water courses appurtenant thereto

v. Not to make any alteration to the demised premises or any part thereof

vi. To pay for all gas, water and electricity used on or in the demised premises

vii. To use the demised premises in a tenant like manner and to keep the interior of the same in a good decorative state of repair and condition

viii. Not to allow any water to overflow from the demised premises to the premises below or adjacent thereto

3. Provided that if the rent or any part thereof shall be in arrears for seven days after the same shall have become due (whether legally demanded or not) or if there shall be any breach of any of the agreements on the part of the Tenant herein contained the Landlord may re-enter upon the demised premises and immediately thereupon this tenancy shall absolutely determine but without prejudice to the other rights and remedies of the Landlord

4. Any notice given by the Tenant shall be given or sent to the Landlord at [address] and any notice given by the Landlord to the Tenant shall be sufficiently served if left at the demised premises or sent by prepaid post to the Tenant at the demised premises. Any notice sent by post shall be deemed to have been served not later than the third day after the posting thereof.

5. The Landlord agrees that in the event of it wishing to dispose of the entire property it will give three months notice in writing of the termination of this tenancy to the Tenant and by the expiry of this term notice (or of any notice given under 1 above) the Tenant will quietly vacate the demised premises giving the Landlord a forwarding address)

AS WITNESS the hands of the parties the day and year first before written

Signed by ....

on behalf of the Landlord in the presence of [witness]

Signed by ....

the Tenant in the presence of [witness]

TENANCY AGREEMENT

It may be easier to terminate domestic residency if the premises are let for a specific term and on a furnished basis, which is anticipated by the following agreement.

AGREEMENT FOR RENTAL OF (property address)

.... (the furnished premises)

made between .... (the Landlord)

of .... (address)

and .... (the tenant)

of .... (address)

on this .... day of .... 199 ....

This Tenancy Agreement for the personal occupation of the above premises is made between the above parties, and comes into effect on .... (the commencement date), and runs for .... months (the term), until .... (the termination date). Following the expiry of this Agreement and with the consent of the parties a fresh Agreement can be entered into.

1. OCCUPATION AND DESCRIPTION. The Parties agree that the Landlord will let and the Tenant will occupy the furnished premises, comprising (number) .... rooms plus bathroom, toilet, (other), for the term, for the purposes of normal domestic residence only.

2. USE AND ABUSE. The tenant may have the reasonable use of the property, furniture and other household effects at the furnished premises as set out on the schedule attached hereto, and will be responsible for any damage and repair (other than that caused by fair wear and tear) to the property, furniture and household effects. The tenant will be entitled to normal use of the house providing it is kept neat and tidy and is cleaned regularly

3. DAMAGE DEPOSIT. On signing this Agreement, the tenant will pay a deposit equal to 20 days charge (see 5 below) to the Landlord to hold against the completion of each requirement in this Agreement, and the return of the property, furniture and household effects in a reasonable condition (fair wear and tear excepted). Such deposit, less any amounts deducted to take account of any damage, replacement, etc., will be returned within 7 days of the termination of this Agreement.

4. OCCUPATION AND ACCESS. The tenant will occupy the property for the term. The Landlord reserves the right of entry during the term for the purposes of inspection, repair, servicing and the access of public utility authorities, reasonable notice (at least 48 hours) being given at all times, other than in an emergency.

5. TENANCY CHARGE. The monthly charge for the tenancy is exclusive of occupation costs (see 6 below) payable on the first of each month in advance by Bankers Order in favour of the Landlord at its bank account at [details]. (Any payment due in respect of an incomplete month will be apportioned on the basis of £ per day.) In the event of any payment being made late, interest at the rate of 2% over base rate from the due date until the date of payment, will be due and must be paid with such late payment.

6. OUTGOINGS. In addition to the payment of the deposit and monthly charge, the tenant will be responsible for all outgoings (including but not restricted to any council tax or equivalent charge, water and sewerage rates, gas, electricity, telephone, etc.) in respect of the premises during the term. The tenant hereby agrees to pay all such amounts immediately an account is rendered, and to indemnify the Landlord in respect of any disputes arising from such payments. On the termination date, the tenant will arrange for any meters to be read, and will provide a forwarding address to all utilities and the local council (as well as to the Landlord) for the submission of their accounts.

7. ABSOLUTE BAR on assignment or parting with possession. The tenant's right of occupation is limited to the term, is personal and cannot under any circumstances be assigned. Possession of the property must not be parted with under any circumstances, neither can any permanent guests be accommodated.

8. BREACH OF AGREEMENT. In the event of three monthly charges being made late, or any outgoing charge being unpaid so that it generates a final demand notice, or the equivalent, the Landlord may treat this Agreement as having been terminated by the Tenant, who must vacate within 14 days of the Landlord's written notice to this effect. In this event all amounts due under this Agreement to the date of such vacation (including interest on late payment plus any losses or costs suffered by the Landlord in respect of the premature termination) must be paid by the Tenant within 7 days of a written demand. In the event of late payment interest as laid down in clause 5 will also be due to the date of payment.

9. INSURANCE AND LIABILITY. The Landlord's insurance covers only the furnished premises and the items set out in the inventory (and any breakage, replacements etc.) thereto. The tenant should take out insurance covering their own possessions situated in or around the house during the duration of this Agreement. Should the premises be damaged by fire, and occupation be impossible for more than a week due to such damage this Agreement will be void, save that the tenant will be responsible for all outgoings and rent up to and including the date of the incident. Should the premises suffer such loss or damage as a result of the tenant's negligence or fault, so that the Landlord's insurance is voided or impaired, the tenant will be liable for such loss or damage. The Landlord or their insurers will accept no liability for loss or damage to the property of the tenant suffered in, or of any injury caused to the tenant or any person visiting or staying in the premises, as a result of such an incident. In the event of the Landlord's insurance premiums being increased solely because of any action or inaction of the tenant, any such increased premium will be regarded as an outgoing and must be paid by the tenant with the next following monthly charge.

10. PETS. The tenant may only keep pet(s) on the premises with the express and prior written permission of the Landlord whose decision as to suitability will be final. Any damage caused by such pet(s) must be properly and adequately repaired.

11. NEIGHBOURS. The tenant is expected to occupy the premises in a sober and responsible manner at all times and must not allow or permit to be done anything which will cause annoyance or disturbance to any neighbour. In the event of the Landlord considering that any act or action is in contravention of this obligation the tenant will cease such act or action immediately.

12. TERMINATION. Unless previously brought to an end, this agreement will end on the termination date, and the tenant will ensure that the Landlord is granted access on that day (or, by mutual agreement between the parties, on an alternative and earlier day) to take possession of the keys and to check the inventory for damage or loss. At least one month before the termination date, the Landlords will serve the notice under the Rent Act 1977, on the tenants at the premises, stating that possession must be granted on the termination date. The tenant will grant vacant possession, and will quietly leave the premises, on or before the termination date.

ONE STOP PROPERTY

Signed .... the Landlord
                   .... Witness

Address

....

Signed .... the Tenant
                   .... Witness

Address ....

....

Termination

Introduction

A lease gives rights of occupation of the premises for a set number of years. It also entails obligations on the part of the lessee to pay for such occupation during that time. Providing the lessee complies with the various covenants in the lease, the landlord will be unable, without the lessee's agreement, to gain vacant possession until the end of the lease and even then only in certain circumstances. Of course, the lessee may wish to be released from the commitment and there are a number of ways in which this can be achieved.

Effluxion of time

This is the phrase given to the coming to the end of the lease in accordance with the expiry of its term. However, even though a lease may state that it is a 20-year lease from 1 January 1978 this does not mean that it will necessary come to an end at midnight on 31 December 1997. As is set out in the section on the LANDLORD AND TENANT ACT, the landlord must take certain action to bring the lease to a close. Similarly, if the landlord has not taken such action, a lessee can initiate such action. This could occur when, for example, rent is protected by an upwards-only clause and a lessee wishes to expose rental negotiations to open market conditions. If the landlord does not initiate action to terminate, the lease simply continues at the existing rent.

Assignment

The lessee could sell his interest to a third party. The danger here, as highlighted in ASSIGNMENT, is that, for leases entered into before 1 January 1996, in selling the right of occupation the lessee does not relinquish liability for the outgoings due under the lease should the assignee default on payment.

Underletting

Strictly speaking, underletting does not terminate the lessee's interest but merely removes their current right of occupation. Underletting can only be entered into if it is allowed by the lease terms and will usually require the landlord's consent. As a means of foregoing the responsibility for paying the outgoings due under a lease, underletting has a number of advantages

(a) the original lessee retains control of the premises and should the underlessee default can take action to regain possession of the premises

(b) the lessee becomes a landlord in their own right and may be able to make a profit on the arrangement. This is unlikely to continue past the lease renewal (if indeed the lessee wants it to) as the superior landlord can require the original lessee to drop out of the chain so that they can issue a new lease direct to the underlessee

(c) granting short-term underlettings can be lucrative whilst retaining the flexibility of knowing one can reoccupy within a short space of time should the business expand.

> **WARNING** Failure to be in occupation when the lease expires will probably mean that the lessee will lose the right of renewal. In the case of *Graysim Holdings Ltd v P&O Property Holdings Ltd* the court held that a landlord was entitled not to grant a new lease to a lessee who was not in occupation.

Buying the freehold interest

The lease will come to an end should the lessee buy the landlord's freehold interest. In this case the MARRIAGE OF INTERESTS may mean that the value of the combined interest is actually more than the sum of the values of the separate interests.

Forfeiture

The lease requires both parties to carry out certain acts and to comply with all the lease COVENANTS. Failure on the part of either party may give the other the right to take action to enforce compliance. Thus in the *British Telecom v Sun Life Assurance* case, the landlord was obliged to keep parts of a property not occupied by the lessee in good repair at all times (i.e. the landlord could not have a 'reasonable time' within which the repairs should be rectified). Repeated failure on the part of the lessee to comply with the covenants (e.g. to pay rent on time, keep the premises in a proper state of repair, etc.) could provide the landlord with an action for breach of covenant and forfeiture. Forfeiture brings occupation to an end, but may not be an end to the lessee's responsibilities for the outgoings.

Options to break

Due to the realisation of the onerous effect of the Privity of Contract rule and the impact of upwards-only rent reviews, in recent years there has been a marked increase in the number of leases incorporating break clauses. These operate to bring the lease to an end much earlier than the full term. Thus a 25-year lease might give an OPTION TO BREAK after five years either to the lessee or to the landlord or to both. Effectively, if both parties have an option they actually only have a five year lease until the option date has passed. If the option is properly exercised and accepted then the lease terminates on the option date and the lessee's obligations end on that date. If the original lessee had assigned their interest and the option was exercised then that is the end of their potential liability under the PRIVITY OF CONTRACT rules.

Surrender

With a depressed property market surrender is relatively rare. It entails the landlord agreeing to take back the premises and effectively cancelling the lease before its expiry. When the property market was buoyant, however, a number of surrenders did occur. With rentals rapidly increasing, some landlords became frustrated having to wait for review patterns of five or seven years or even longer to gain the benefit of these increases in rents chargeable. Accordingly, a number of deals were made with lessees whereby lower rented property was surrendered (effectively the lease was 'bought in') so that it could be relet possibly on a three year rent review pattern at an inflated initial rent.

The prospective deal needs to be very advantageous since the landlord loses not just a lessee but also the value of the contingent liability of that lessee, as some landlords have since found to their cost. When the property market slumped, many of the new lessee whose businesses were often "high risk" in nature, saw their trade collapse and went into liquidation, leaving the landlords with empty properties and without recourse.

Terrorist Action

Introduction

Organisations, can become subject to loss and injury as a result of terrorist activity. In recognition of this fact, organisations should have a policy for dealing with telephone threats and suspect packages, even if, to avoid undue concern, the contents are made known to only a few employees. Conversely, some organisations, being more prone to such threats, may need to alert their staff by distributing the policy widely. Often the responsibility for this aspect of security will devolve to the property administrator.

Telephone threats

Most threats are made over the telephone and the police estimate that over 95% are hoaxes, often, as far as employers are concerned, carried out by disaffected employees or ex-employees. Indeed, the percentage of hoaxes may be higher as many such calls are not reported. Receptionists and telephonists should be coached to deal with such calls in the following manner.

Dealing with threat by telephone

1. Accept the call in a calm, unhurried manner. Ask caller to repeat the sentence or message to give yourself time to recover and possibly, without alerting the caller, to advise someone who can listen in.

2. Try to keep caller talking for example, invent phrases such as 'I'm sorry this is a bad line I can't hear you clearly', or 'I don't understand what you mean, could you repeat that please so that I get it right?' or 'Did you say (repeat the statement the caller made)?' etc.

3. Find out as much information as possible. Take particular note of any unusual or repeated words or phrases used in case these contain a code word.

4. Try to find out the answers to the following questions:

(a) Is there a bomb, and if so where is it?

(b) What type is it – explosive, gas, etc?

(c) Who put it there, and when?

(d) Who are you? What organisation do you represent?

(e) Do you have a police identification code?

(f) When will the bomb go off?

(g) Why are you taking this action against the organisation?

(h) Do you have a grudge against this organisation?

(i) What is the nature of your complaint?

(j) Will the bomb affect fire evacuation routes?

Note   If it will, do not activate the fire alarm as this could put employees at greater risk).

5. During, or immediately after, the conversation make a note of the caller's characteristics. In particular, note the following:

   (a) Whether the caller seemed young, old, male, female, British, foreign.

   (b) Special accent or speech defect.

   (c) Drunk or drugged, lucid, rambling or incoherent.

   (d) Did it sound as if message was being read.

   (e) Whether there were any background noises, or anything else of note, e.g. a train announcement or echo.

6. Notify a senior member of staff during the call or immediately after. Senior person will need to make decision whether to evacuate or not, and will contact police/fire service. Before arranging evacuation, fire evacuation routes should be checked for any suspicious packages. If suspicious packages are found, an alternative means of escape should be used. If not, use fire escape routes to evacuate.

   Note   The police may advise not to use the fire alarm as noise may set off some devices).

   Staff should be requested to take personal belongings with them, to avoid wasting time on identifying innocent packages during the police search.

TERRORIST ACTION

7. When the police arrive, staff should act in accordance with their instructions. The police will normally request that an employee accompany them during the search to identify, and thus eliminate, harmless packages.

   Note   *Organisations with a record of such alarms should arrange to link a tape recorder to the switchboard ready for immediate operation.)*

Suspect packages

Whilst threat calls are usually hoaxes and in any event give some time for reaction, the receipt of a suspect package brings the potential danger into the premises without warning. Staff whose responsibility it is to handle post should be coached in the following manner.

Dealing with suspect packages

1. The organisation will publish regularly a list of countries from which suspect packages could arrive. All packages from these countries should be treated with caution.

2. All packages which are oddly addressed, show signs of staining from a liquid, display metal protrusions, seem to contain machinery not likely to be of interest to the recipient, have broken coverings, have contents which are ticking (or making a similar noise), smell of almonds or marzipan, etc., (this list is not meant to be exhaustive) should be treated with considerable suspicion and placed within the secure section in the post room.

3. The department, and surrounding departments, should be cleared, the matter should be reported to the senior manager present, and the police should be summoned.

Liability

It should not be overlooked that an organisation's liability insurers have an interest in this matter and need to be kept informed particularly of the following:

(a) if employees regularly accompany police when checking for suspect packages

(b) the organisation has decided to ignore bomb warning calls (and thus employees do not evacuate the building on receipt of a telephone threat)

(c) The organisation leaves the decision of whether to evacuate or not to the individual employee in such circumstances.

Toilet Facilities

> **Introduction**
>
> The provision of sufficient toilet facilities is required under the Workplace (Health Safety and Welfare) Regulations 1992 which came into effect on 1 January 1993. Premises in existence on January 1993 had until December 1996 to comply, but new premises are required to provide the facilities immediately.

The requirements

Employers are required to provide the facilities stated depending on the numbers employed in each location.

Employees	Water closets	Wash stations
1–5	1	1
6–25	2	2
26–50	3	3
51–75	4	4
76–100	5	5
thereafter for every additional 25 employees	1	1

> *Note* These facilities are required for each sex and once the number of employees breaks a threshold (e.g. 101, 126), the requirement is for the next higher number of facilities.)

For toilet facilities provided solely for men, the employer can provide (in addition to the wash stations as stated above) either the water closet facilities set out above or the following:

Male employees	Water closets	Urinals
1–15	1	1
16–45	2	2
46–75	3	3
76–100	4	4
thereafter for every additional 25 employers	1	

but every fourth additional WC can be replaced by 1 urinal.

> *Note* Again, once the number of men employed breaks a threshold, the next higher number of facilities must be provided.

The approved code of practice (sanitary and washing facilities) re Workplace (Health, Safety and Welfare) Regulations 1992 is available from HMSO and should be referred to.

Trespassers

Introduction

Anyone who does not work, has not been invited or has no official right to be on premises can be regarded as a trespasser or, if they seem to have taken up residence, as a squatter. However although trespassers or squatters have no right to be on the premises, their presence cannot be ignored. If there is a chance that trespassers can venture on to or into the premises then their safety must be taken into account. (see OCCUPIER'S LIABILITY).

Prevention

It is perhaps stating the obvious to state that efforts should be made to make premises and land secure so that casual access is rendered difficult, but nevertheless experience indicates that all too often too little is done to make it clear that access is allowed to authorised personnel only through designated entrances and at certain times. Thus boundary walls and fences should be kept in good repair and defensive measures (high walls surmounted by barrier wire, etc.) installed, gates should be sturdy and kept locked, notices should be displayed stating that not only is access denied to the unauthorised but also that there is danger to unauthorised persons from illegal entry. If security is a major issue, additional safeguards such as security inspections and/or closed circuit television could be installed although the expense that either of these items entail may militate against this. As in all things, the potential loss needs to be compared with the costs of the added protection.

Hazards

Despite notices warning of danger, however, the occupier is not absolved from liability if a trespasser, particularly a child, is injured on the premises. Hazards such as wells, ladders and flat roofs may also need to be guarded. In addition, the use of guard dogs to improve security, unless under supervision or on leash, may pose a hazard.

Squatters

Whereas most trespassers remain on the property for a relatively short period – either to attempt to steal from or cause damage to the property, or, as far as children are concerned simply to play there – squatters tend to occupy the premises or part of them on a long term basis. They can prove difficult to eject and specific advice needs to be taken in such circumstances. It should not be assumed that simply because they have no right to be there that they can be ejected. A court order is usually needed to evict them.

> <u>Note</u> In the case of Margereson & Hancock v J W Roberts Ltd, the company was held to be liable to the widow of a man who had contracted a disease as a result of him playing, when a child, in the asbestos-ridden dust of their loading bay – where he had no right to be. Property occupiers need to be proactive to ensure trespassers' safety is maximised and their own liability is minimised.

Underletting

Introduction

Agreeing to the contract implicit in a lease is a long term commitment for both landlord and lessee. Whilst it is true that the lessee can cut short this commitment by assigning their interest, the danger for the original lessee is that, for leases entered into before 1 January 1996, should the assignee (or a subsequent assignee) default the original assignee could be left to fund the outgoings due under the lease to the landlord with no right of re-entry and re-occupation of the premises (see PRIVITY OF CONTRACT). As an alternative, lessees could consider underletting.

Basis

The basis of an underlease is that all the responsibilities of the original lessee are passed on to an underlessee who will also benefit, at the lessee's discretion, from some of the rights under the lease. In addition, it is normal for the term allowed to an underlessee to be slightly shorter than that to which the lessee is entitled. This is a practical precaution taken to try to ensure that vacant possession can be given when the original lease expires, if the underlease terminates a month before the lease, the original lessee has the opportunity to ensure the underlessee has not only left the premises but also left it in a reasonable condition before the due date that they must vacate.

Permission

A lessee has no automatic right to underlet the premises. Indeed, many lessees will actually be prohibited from doing so as their lease will either contain a covenant requiring them, to remain in occupation (other than for short periods) or prohibiting them from underletting at all. Providing, however, that there is a clause allowing underletting 'with the permission of the landlord, such permission not to be unreasonably withheld' then the lessee will need to submit full details of the proposed underlessee for approval to the landlord. Normally the landlord will wish to see evidence of financial reliability and to be assured that the organisation or person is likely to be a responsible and reasonable tenant and one that will keep the premises in a reasonable state, etc. Indeed, these requirements are in the interests of the original lessee as well as those of the landlord and so should have already been investigated.

A deed granting the landlord's permission to the underletting will be prepared requiring as parties the landlord, the lessee and the proposed underlessee. Such a deed may require the underlessee to comply with all the terms in the original lease and may even recite all such terms.

Underletting the whole only

Normally a lessee will be able to underlet only the whole premises as an entity. Unless the premises are large and easily sub divided, it may not be in anyone's interest to consider underletting parts of the property to different underlessees. Without experienced property management available close at hand, unrestricted partial underletting can lead to unauthorised underlettings and sub-subtenancies. The difficulty in this situation is not only understanding the relationships between underlessees but also regaining vacant possession. In addition, the responsibility for repairs and redecorations tends to be unclear. A casual attitude to underletting may tend to inculcate a casual attitude to the responsibilities of occupation.

Lessee removal

Where an underletting has been arranged with the landlord's permission, and particularly where a profit rent has been obtained, if may be possible for the landlord to require the original lessee to drop out of the relationship at the termination of the lease. In such a case the landlord can negotiate new lease terms direct with the underlessee thus acquiring the benefit of the enhanced rent. This was the decision in the recent case of *Graysim Holdings Ltd v P&O Property Holdings Ltd*. Because the tenant had sublet the areas, the House of Lords found that they then had no protected holding when the landlord served notice ending the business letting.

Use and User Clause

Introduction

Even if it is freehold, the use to which a property can be put is constrained by planning considerations which may restrict such matters as hours of work should, for example, a factory be located within a residential area. If the property is leasehold, use may be constrained by a user clause and any trading restrictions contained in the lease (e.g. some leases prohibit the use of the premises to sell alcohol, conduct auctions, etc.) as well as by local planners.

Operation

When negotiating lease terms an executive with intimate knowledge of the operation of the business should check the impact of any and all restrictions on the operation of the business that are included (see COVENANTS).

Case study

A service business was negotiating a new lease. Included in the lease was a requirement that the business should be open (and only open) between the hours of 8 a.m. and 6 p.m. on Monday to Saturday. To many service-orientated businesses these hours might have caused no problem. However the business being carried on was that of supplying and hiring wedding apparel and ancillary services. Not only was there no need and no intention to open before 11.00 a.m. each morning but also the main business was conducted between 4 p.m. and 8 p.m. on the weekdays and Saturdays and also for a few hours on Sunday. Hence the apparently innocuous restrictions on the use of the property via the authorised hours of business would have had a crippling effect on the business had these not been challenged.

Planning use

Generally, the classification of uses under the Town and Country Planning

(Use classes) Order 1987 is as follows.

Only a brief outline of items under each class has been given in the following list.

Class A1 – Retailing of items for sale generally

Class A2 – Provision of services

Class A3 – Provision of food

Class B1 – Office, research and industrial use without detriment to the environment

Class B2 – Industrial use other than that included in B1

Class B3 – Industrial use as defined by the Alkali Works Regulations 1906

Class B4 – Industrial use (smelting, galvanising, etc.)

Class B5 – Industrial use (bricks, crushing, fuel ash, etc.)

Class B6 – Industrial use (oil, stoving, rubber, chemicals, etc.)

Class B7 – Industrial use (boiling, fish, skins, fats, etc.)

Class B8 – Storage and distribution

Class C1 – Hotels

Class C2 – Residential homes, hospitals, etc.

Class C3 – Residential houses

Class D1 – Non-residential premises (day nurseries, libraries, etc.)

Class D2 – Assembly and leisure premises (cinemas, theatres, dance halls, swimming baths, etc.)

Premises are not permitted, without a variation, to be used for a use other than that for which they are designated.

User clauses

In addition to restrictions applied under planning laws as set out above, many leases include clauses that stipulate the purpose for which the premises covered by the lease are intended. This is particularly relevant to retailing, but office and warehouse leases can also be restrictive.

It is important on agreeing terms that the full purposes for which the premises will be used are included in any user clause. If this is not the case and the premises are then used for a purpose other than that as specified, then the lessee will be in breach of the covenants under the lease.

Normally, if there is a user clause, alterations to it are allowed to be made subject to the permission of the landlord. The restrictive nature of this is often alleviated by the addition of words such as 'such permission not to be unreasonably withheld'. In practice, this has allowed some landlords to negotiate additional rent when a request for additional use was made on the basis that if the rent agreed was fair for the use agreed then any additional use should attract greater rent. For example, when the National Lottery outlets were authorised some landlords attempted to increase the rent being paid arguing that it was an extension of permitted use.

Effect on rent review

There may be some logic in a landlord attempting to gain additional rent in exchange for allowing the premises for additional uses provided that when the rent was originally agreed the equal logic that a lease with a restricted user clause should command a lower rent than a lease for premises covered by an unrestricted user clause. The logic of restricted user clauses equalling restricted rent should also hold good when it comes to rent review and any wording such as 'any restricted user clause is to be ignored in assessing the rent to be paid on review' should be deleted. Lessees who use premises for purposes other than those that are allowed by their lease are in breach of the lease and may find their rights, etc. under the lease are impaired or, ultimately, that they lose the right of occupation by forfeiture.

Valuations

Introduction

In many organisations, other than the skills of their employees, their property may be among the most valuable assets of the business. If this is the case then the true value of such assets should be known by the business. If the value is not known appropriate decisions concerning the assets cannot be made.

Staged valuation

Many property owners adopt as a policy the concept of revaluing (say) a third of their portfolio every year meaning that over a period of three years their whole portfolio will be updated. Not only does this mean that at any time the value of none should be more than three years out of date but also it spreads the cost of the valuations. If a system of recharging the businesses using the premises with a current market rent is adopted (see OBTAINING VALUE), the valuations themselves can serve as a base for the calculation of these rents. In this way, a figure related to the value of the property in a particular location is available and applied.

As an alternative, staged revaluations over a five-year period can be used, although property values tend to be somewhat dynamic and to leave a valuation of part of the portfolio for five years may mean that some valuations are seriously out of date.

Instruction

For valuations to be reliable and of use, for example, in the financial books of the organisation, it will be necessary to retain suitably qualified surveyors or valuers to conduct the work. If such advisers regularly carry out work for the organisation, and/or a commitment to repeat the process regularly is made, it may be possible to negotiate a reduced fee. Certainly at the time of the second or subsequent valuation the fee should be reduced if the same adviser is used as a certain amount of information and knowledge of the property will have already been assimilated and be available.

Other matters

As part of a valuation, particularly one in advance of a decision to purchase, checks can also be made on floor loadings, security, and energy supplies as well as the exact position of boundaries. Some firms can also provide valuations of plant and machinery. For the purposes of insurance cover it may be necessary to obtain valuations although here it is normally the cost of rebuilding that may be required (see also SURVEYS).

Case references

Adams v Southern Electricity Board (1994 Court of Appeal)

British Telecom v Sun Life Assurance (Times 3.8.95)

Co-op v Argyll Stores (1996 9 EG 128)

Graysim Holdings Ltd v P & O Property Holdings Ltd (Times 24.11.95)

Hampson t/a Abbey Self Storage v Newcastle upon Tyne (Times 31.1.96)

Havenbridge Ltd v Boston Dyers Ltd (Times 1.4.96)

Jervis v Harris (1996 10 EG 159)

Margereson & Hancock v JW Roberts Ltd (Times 17.4.96)

Meade Hill and anor v The British Council (4.95 Court of Appeal)

R v Gateway Foodmarkets Ltd (Times 2.1.97)

R v Rhone Poulenc Rorer Ltd (TLR 1.12.95)

Retail Parks Investments Ltd v Royal Bank of Scotland (Times 22.4.96)